The Cupcake Cookbook

Other books by Laurence Sombke:

Fearless Entertaining
Omelettes: Eggs at Their Best
Glorious Roots

The Cupcake Cookbook

More than 70 Recipes for
Easy, Delicious Cupcakes and Frostings

Catherine Herman and Laurence Sombke

• • •

ST. MARTIN'S PRESS ♦ NEW YORK

Library of Congress Cataloging-in-Publication Data

Herman, Catherine.
    The cupcake cookbook / Catherine Herman and Laurence Sombke.
        p.   cm.
    ISBN 0-312-09265-2
    1. Cake.   I. Sombke, Laurence.   II. Title.
TX771.S55   1993
641.8'653—dc20   93-900
                                                    CIP

First Edition: July 1993

10 9 8 7 6 5 4 3 2 1

To our children, Henry and Kit, the sweetest little cupcakes in the whole wide world.

Thanks, Mom and Dad, for all your support and for giving us the Mixmaster that helped us test all these recipes. And thanks, Laurie McCredie, for introducing us to the Ice Cream Cone Cupcake and for so lovingly looking after our children while we wrote this book.

Contents

Introduction   1
The History of Cupcakes   3
Baking the Perfect Cupcake   7
    Equipment   8
    Ingredients and Cupcake Chemistry   12
    Basic Cupcake Technique   17
    Common Baking Terms   20
    Frosting and Decorating Tips   21
Cupcakes and Kids   25
Dinner Party Cupcakes   61
Chocolate Cupcakes   77
Fruit and Nut Cupcakes   91
Coffee Cake Cupcakes   105
Healthy Cupcakes   119
Index   130

The Cupcake Cookbook

Introduction

As the parents of two young children, we found ourselves baking a lot of cupcakes. School parties, birthday parties, and family gatherings summoned us into the kitchen to whip up those fanciful portions of frosted cake.

Growing tired of the traditional chocolate cupcake with white frosting and its counterpart, the yellow cupcake with chocolate frosting, we began experimenting. What about cream-filled cupcakes? No. Too much trouble, we thought. We had visions of pastry bags and gooey cream oozing all over our kitchen with messy results. Over time, however, we discovered some terrifically trouble-free, filled cupcake recipes like moist Coconut Cream–filled Chocolate Cupcakes or Peanut Butter–Filled Chocolate Cupcakes that both kids and adults love to eat.

We began adapting classic cake recipes like German chocolate cake and pineapple upside-down cake into cupcake concepts. What fun at a dinner party to present a platter of assorted cupcakes ranging from elegant Black Forest Cupcakes to Pineapple Orange Cupcakes to Lemon Meringue Cupcakes.

We discovered that we could freeze cupcakes. Let them defrost an hour before they're needed, ice them, and—voilà!—homemade cupcakes in a pinch. Best of all, cupcakes became a fun family activity. Our son, Henry, loves to help put the paper liners in the muffin tins, make the batter and frosting, and, of course, lick the spoons. He also enjoys the creativity of decorating the cupcakes or putting the chocolate kiss in the center of the batter as a special chocolate surprise.

This book shares all of our wonderful cupcake discoveries and demonstrates the ease with which cupcakes can be made and decorated. So roll up your sleeves, put on an apron, and get ready to have some good old-fashioned fun with cupcakes.

The History of Cupcakes

The origin of the cupcake somehow escaped the scrutiny of food historians, and there is very little written about how this tasty treat came into existence.

The earliest record we can find for a cupcake recipe is in the 1896 first edition of Fanny Merritt Farmer's Boston Cooking-School Cook Book. The recipe instructs the reader to bake the cakes in individual tin cups but does not call for the fluted paper liners that have come to define cupcakes as we know them today.

So when did these novel bake cups come into existence? We believe they were introduced by the commercial baking industry just after World War I.

Dale Motes, a product manager for the James River Corporation, a Michigan-based major manufacturer of cupcake liners, says that many of the machines they use to manufacture bake cups were originally designed to make artillery shells during World War I. After the war, the machinery was adapted to crimp paper for the fluted bake cups and are still in use today. It's comforting to know that equipment used to make bullets has been transformed to create something as harmless as fluted cupcake papers.

Jerry Shapiro, a fifty-year veteran of the bake cup industry and account executive at Bleyer Industries, another major manufacturer of bake cups, says that the fluted bake cup has been around for at least seventy-five years. According to Mr. Shapiro, there were two reasons commercial bakeries adopted the use of paper liners. First, they saved bakers from the time-consuming task of cleaning the pans and, second, they provided a sanitary and convenient means for handling the small cakes. Soon after their introduction to the commercial baking industry, the fluted liners became available in grocery stores and widely used by home bakers.

We believe that the idea to use fluted cups in baking originated with the

German bakers who founded many of the original commercial bakeries in the United States such as Entenmann's, Dugans, and Freihofers. It is likely that in the 1920s the Germans, who were well known for their fine confections and candy, adapted the miniature fluted candy cups for use in the baking of cupcakes.

The earliest cupcakes made by commercial bakers were much the same as they are today, variations on basic yellow or chocolate cakes with chocolate or white frosting. The origins of fancier cupcakes, such as Drake's Yankee Doodles or Hostess's Cream Filled Cupcakes, are unclear because the companies have no archival records of their introduction. The best estimate is that these cakes reached the market some time before World War II.

So there you have it. A history of the cupcake—short and sweet.

Baking the
Perfect Cupcake

Anyone can bake cupcakes. Everyone should bake cupcakes. They're easy and fun to make. They're simpler to frost than large layer cakes. And they're delicious to eat. Kids love cupcakes, parents and grandparents love to bake cupcakes for kids and then eat a few themselves. Teachers see lots of cupcakes, we're sure.

It's easy to turn out moist, flavorful cupcakes every time you bake. Just follow the hints about equipment, ingredients, and technique found in this chapter and your cupcake baking will be more efficient and trouble-free.

EQUIPMENT

You don't need a lot of fancy baking equipment to make cupcakes. Aside from the muffin pan and paper cupcake liners, which give these cakes their distinguishing characteristics, common basic utensils like spatulas, bowls, mixers, measuring cups, and spoons are essentially what you need. The one less common item we recommend is an oven thermometer. It's the most inexpensive investment you'll make for good baking results.

Muffin pans. Muffin pans come in three basic sizes: miniature, standard, and jumbo, or "Texas-style."

Pans made of heavy-gauge metals give the best results.

Miniature pans are roughly 1⅝ inches in diameter, ⅝ inch deep, and hold ¾ fluid ounce. These tiny forms bake wonderful bite-size cupcakes, making tidy little treats for toddler birthday parties.

Standard pans are roughly 2¾ inches in diameter, 1¼ inches deep, and hold 3¼ fluid ounces. This is the most common pan available and holds about ½ cup of batter when full. These typically come with either 6- or 12-cup forms. Since most of the recipes in this book are for 12 or more cupcakes, select 12-cup pans or at least 2 6-cup pans.

Jumbo, or Texas-Style, pans are roughly 3½ inches in diameter, 1¼ inches deep, and hold 6 fluid ounces. This pan became popular with the advent of the muffin craze that swept the country in the 1980s. The cup forms, as indicated in the pan's name, are quite large, holding nearly double the amount of batter in a standard cupcake pan. Jumbo bake cup liners are available in most grocery stores. Although the notion of jumbo cupcakes is fun, I find them awkward and difficult to handle, especially for little hands. They could easily serve two, but then who wants to share his cupcake with someone else?

Cupcake liners. Cupcake liners, or bake cups, are available in many sizes and colors. Fluted paper bake cups sold in boxes of assorted colors are the most common. Some can be found in brighter "designer" colors or with printed holiday patterns on them. There are even environmentally friendly liners made from unbleached paper. Foil and heavy aluminum cups are also available and help preserve freshness.

The most important thing to remember when purchasing bake cups is that they should fit properly into the cups of your pan. I once bought a package of "mini" bake cups that were too large for my miniature-size muffin pan. Of course I didn't discover this until the batter was prepared and ready to pour into the cups. So if you're deviating from the standard size bake cup, know the dimensions of your pan.

Bowls. I like to have several bowls of varying sizes on hand when I bake: a small bowl for sifting and measuring flour; a medium bowl for combining all dry ingredients such as flour, baking powder, and salt; another small bowl for separating and beating egg whites; and, of course, the main large bowl in which I cream together the butter and sugar and then combine the other ingredients.

Sifter. I have two sifters, a small squeeze-handle sifter and a larger crank-handle sifter. I prefer the smaller one because I can dip it into my flour canister and scoop out the quantity I need. However, if you have a little helper in the kitchen, like my five-year-old son, Henry, who enjoys sifting flour as much as playing in the sandbox, a crank-handle sifter is much easier for small hands to operate.

Liquid measuring cups. Liquid measuring cups are typically spout-shaped cups with handles, convenient for pouring. I prefer the glass, heatproof cups such as the Pyrex brand over plastic measuring cups.

Solid measuring cups. Solid measuring cups come in sets of four separate cups (¼ cup, ⅓ cup, ½ cup, and 1 cup) that stack inside one another.

Measuring spoons. Measuring spoons are available in plastic or stainless steel and typically have four spoons per set (¼ teaspoon, ½ teaspoon, 1 teaspoon, and 1 tablespoon).

Electric mixers. There are two types of electric mixers: the stationary stand mixer and the hand mixer. A powerful hand mixer will generally handle any batter and frosting recipe in this book. However, I enjoy using my stationary mixer for batters and egg whites and my hand mixer for beating frostings on the stove top.

Spatulas. Rubber spatulas come in various shapes and sizes to fit different size bowls and different types of substances. They are handy for scraping the sides of bowls, for mixing, for folding in egg whites, and for spreading frostings. Metal spatulas are specifically intended for frosting cakes. For cupcakes, the smaller the metal spatula, the better the results. Depending on the effect I'm trying to create, I sometimes resort to using the back of a teaspoon.

Small ladle. Although not essential, a small soup ladle comes in handy for filling the cupcake liners with batter. A large serving spoon is also useful.

Oven and oven thermometer. I believe that these go hand in hand. It's virtually impossible to bake cupcakes without an oven, and without an oven thermometer it's impossible to know whether your oven's thermostat is accurate. If you're taking the time to prepare the batter, why not reward yourself by baking it at the proper temperature?

Wire racks. Wire racks help your cupcakes cool properly when you first take them out of the oven and after you remove them from the pan. Have at least two rectangular racks available when baking cupcakes.

Cake tester. I use my finger and a wooden toothpick to test for doneness. First I touch the cupcake while it's still in the oven to see if the cake is firm enough for the toothpick test. If it is still sticky or moist to the touch, I leave it in the oven a bit longer. If it is firm and bounces back to my touch, I remove the pan from the oven and insert a toothpick in the center. If the toothpick comes out clean, the cupcakes are done.

INGREDIENTS AND CUPCAKE CHEMISTRY

Though we seldom think of it as such, baking is chemistry. Ingredients are blended and heated to cause chemical reactions and result in some of the most delicious science experiments man has ever tasted.

My young son, Henry, was excited to discover the science side of baking when I asked him to test the baking powder for freshness. To do this, you mix 1 teaspoon of baking powder with ⅓ cup warm water. If it fizzes, the baking powder is good. The fizzing is the release of carbon dioxide gas, which, in baking terms, means the cake is expanding and being leavened.

The point I'm getting at is that all your ingredients should be fresh, or you won't get the proper chemical reactions you need to bake attractive, good-tasting cupcakes.

Flour. Most of the recipes in this book call for all-purpose flour or cake flour. I prefer the more delicate finer-textured results from cake flour, but have found that it is not widely available in grocery stores. Quite often it is available only as self-rising cake flour and you can never be sure if the leavening in it is fresh. Here are two easy formulas for converting all-purpose flour to cake flour. Both work equally well and will save you a trip to the store when you don't have cake flour on hand:

1. 1 cup sifted all-purpose flour = 1 cup + 2 tablespoons sifted cake flour.

2. For each cup of flour used in the recipe, substitute 2 tablespoons cornstarch for 2 tablespoons flour.

Always sift your flour. Ignore all package claims of presifted flour. All flour settles and compacts on the shelf and it needs to be sifted again so that it blends well with the other ingredients and so that your cake will be nice and moist.

Liquids. "Liquids" include milk, eggs, cream, yogurt, sour cream, melted butter, honey, and molasses. They are important ingredients because they add flavor and contain H_2O, better known as water. What happens to water molecules when you heat them? They start jumping around, creating friction and disturbing the air bubbles you beat into the batter. The air bubbles explode and the water molecules release steam, all causing your cupcakes to rise. Who said cupcake batter was boring?

Eggs. Eggs are considered one of the most important ingredients in cake batter, not only for their nutritional value, namely protein, but also for the structure, moisture, color, flavor, and richness they add.

The size of your eggs is important. *Use large eggs at room temperature.*

Room-temperature eggs combine better with shortening when making the cake batter. There are varying opinions, however, about egg whites and whether they achieve fuller volume when beaten chilled or at room temperature. I have beaten egg whites at both temperatures and have achieved equal results.

Many of the recipes in this book call for the eggs to be separated. Leftover egg whites can be covered and stored, and refrigerated for up to one month. Whites and yolks can be frozen separately and then thawed before use. Do not refreeze eggs because they will spoil.

Fat. For the best flavor and texture, use fresh, sweet, unsalted butter. Salted butter tends to make salty-flavored cupcakes. Margarine can be used as a substitute if you're trying to reduce the fat or cholesterol in your recipe. There is no calorie difference between butter or margarine, and arguably butter contributes better flavor. Always use bar or stick butter as opposed to whipped butter, which contains more air. Use cooking oil if the recipe calls for it. Solid shortening, such as Crisco, can be substituted for butter or margarine, but remember it is flavorless, so your cupcakes will lack that certain "something" unless they are robustly flavored with chocolate, molasses, or spices.

Remember! Always bring your fats to room temperature before mixing or your cupcakes will bake up flat and ugly.

Sugar. Sugar, of course, is what makes your cupcakes sweet and helps them stay fresh and moist. Use granulated sugar for the recipes in this book unless otherwise stated. Brown sugar should be fresh, soft, moist, and lump-free. Firmly pack brown sugar in the cup when measuring. Confectioners' sugar, primarily used in frostings and meringues, should be sifted before use.

Leavening. There are two basic leavenings used in this book, baking soda and baking powder. Both have the ability to release carbon dioxide gas, helping your cupcake batter to expand and rise. The chemistry involved is simple: Baking soda (sodium bicarbonate) is a neutralizing agent for acidic foods such as buttermilk, sour cream, yogurt, and cocoa. It is the chemical reaction between baking soda's neutralizing agent, alkaline, and the food's acid agents that releases carbon dioxide gas. Baking powder contains baking soda and acid. Adding moisture causes the two to react, thereby releasing a small amount of carbon dioxide gas. When the batter is placed in the oven, heat makes the gas cells expand and also causes more carbon dioxide to be released. Baking powder loses potency quickly, so it's wise to buy it in small quantities and replace it after about three months. It is relatively inexpensive and is often the unsuspected culprit when cupcakes turn out flat and less than attractive. To test for freshness, mix 1 teaspoon baking powder with ⅓ cup warm water. If the mixture fizzes, the baking powder is fresh. The fizzing is the release of carbon dioxide gas.

Extracts. Vanilla extract is by far the flavoring used most often in cake recipes. This is because vanilla tastes so good and helps to enhance other flavors. Pure vanilla extract is the highly concentrated oil extracted from the vanilla bean. The oil is preserved in alcohol and packaged in dark brown bottles to protect it from bright light, which can cause it to become volatile.

As with all extracts, "pure" is preferred over "imitation." Pure extracts have stronger flavors and hold up better in the baking process. They cost more, but are worth the extra expense.

Zest. Orange and lemon zest, or peels, are two of my favorite flavorings. They're accessible to the average baker, offer superbly strong natural flavor to frostings and cake batter, and can be used for cupcake decorating. For the best flavor use the brightest-colored part of the peel and avoid the bitter-tasting white pith. Accumulate zest either by grating the citrus or by using a vegetable peeler and a sharp knife to mince it.

Chocolate. This all-time favorite is used both to flavor and to decorate cupcakes. The three most commonly used chocolates in baking are squares of unsweetened and semisweet chocolate, and unsweetened cocoa powder. Unsweetened and semisweet chocolate are available in boxes of 1-ounce squares. These are good items to keep on hand and will keep indefinitely if stored in a cool dark place. Unsweetened cocoa powder typically comes in cans. There are two varieties, the regular 100 percent cocoa and the "dutched" or "European" cocoa, which is alkalized.

Nuts. Any nut can be used in baking, but favorites are almonds, walnuts, peanuts, and cashews. Nuts are nutritious, high-protein foods packed with vitamins and minerals. Freshly shelled nuts will give you the best flavor but take more time to prepare. For convenience, it helps to keep a supply of shelled nuts in the freezer, ready to use.

Fruit. Fresh or dried, fruit imparts some of the coziest flavors in baking. When using canned fruit, be sure to drain it properly so as not to include more liquid than the recipe calls for. Dried fruits, such as raisins, apricots, and prunes, should be moist and not hard. Revive stale, hard fruit by simmering it in water for no more than 10 minutes. Drain and pat dry before use.

BASIC CUPCAKE TECHNIQUE

Here's a basic rundown on what you need to know when baking cupcakes. Most instruction manuals, whether for a complicated bicycle assembly or a simple cupcake recipe, tell you to read all the instructions first. This seems like common sense, but sometimes we have a tendency to drive into the unknown. Our blind ambition can cost us hours of frustration and dozens of lousy cupcakes. If you do want to save time and get good results, then, simply, *Read the recipe first!*

1. *Review your recipe and set out all your ingredients and baking equipment.* Never start a recipe without knowing first that you have all the ingredients. Be sure to bring all your chilled ingredients to room temperature. Test to make sure your baking powder is fresh. Locate all the baking equipment you will need to complete the recipe.

2. *Preheat your oven.* Always allow 10 to 15 minutes for your oven

to preheat. *Use an oven thermometer* and adjust the thermostat, if necessary, to compensate for too high or too low oven temperatures.

3. *Prepare your baking pans.* It's important to get your pans out and prepare them for baking before you start mixing the batter. Nothing is more frustrating than discovering you don't have enough cupcake liners after the batter is already prepared. Batters with beaten egg whites lose their volume if left sitting too long before baking.

   If you're not using liners, properly grease and flour your pans. Use vegetable shortening to smear a thin, even film on the bottom and sides of each cup. Dust with flour, one cup at a time, by placing a teaspoon of flour in each cup and turning and shaking the pan. Invert the pan and give the bottom a hard knock to eliminate excess flour.

4. *Measure your ingredients accurately.* Use the appropriate standard measuring cups and spoons for measuring dry and liquid ingredients. If the instructions call for sifted dry ingredients, sift first and then measure them using the flat side of a knife to level the ingredient in the measuring cup.

5. *Blend your ingredients properly and in sequence.* Remember, baking is chemistry and recipes are formulas that must be followed carefully to achieve the proper results. Overmixing can toughen the flour's gluten, causing long tunnels and cracked surfaces. Undermixing can result in crumbly, flat-topped cupcakes with slightly sunken centers.

6. *Fill your pans to the correct height.* Typically, each cup should be filled approximately two-thirds full, allowing room for the cake to rise without spilling over the sides. Fruit, pound, and fudge cupcakes may be filled higher, since these cakes do not rise as much. Fill unused cups halfway with warm water.

7. *Position pan in the center of the oven,* allowing the heat to circulate freely around it. If placing more than one pan in at a time, leave at least 1 inch between pans and between the pan and the oven wall. Ideally, it is best to place cake pans on only one oven rack, but if you do use two, stagger the pans so they are not directly above or below each other.

8. *Do not overbake cupcakes.* Dry crumbly cakes are the result of too much baking. Check cupcakes approximately 5 minutes before the suggested baking time is complete.

9. *Cool cupcakes properly.* When your cupcakes are baked, remove them from the oven and place on wire racks. Allow the cupcakes to cool and settle in the pan, usually 5 to 10 minutes, or as long as the recipe suggests. Then turn the pans over and remove the cupcakes to the rack in an upright position. Cool completely before frosting, unless recipe directs otherwise. To beat egg whites, see Eggs (page 13).

10. Cupcakes can be easily stored or frozen when thoroughly cool. Keep cupcakes fresh for two to three days by placing toothpicks in tops of cakes and covering with plastic wrap. Freeze cupcakes by wrap-

ping in plastic wrap and storing in plastic bags or rubber airtight containers. It is best to freeze unfrosted cupcakes and frosting separately. Thaw by keeping cupcakes wrapped until they reach room temperature. Freeze frosting in airtight plastic container, then thaw to room temperature. Butter cakes generally freeze well for 6 to 12 months. Angel food and sponge cakes freeze well for about 2 months.

COMMON BAKING TERMS

Beat. Beating is accomplished either by hand (using a spoon) or with an electric mixer. To beat by hand, use a long-handled wooden or metal spoon and mix rapidly with a rhythmic, circular motion until the mixture is smooth and light.

Blend. To combine one ingredient with another, by hand or with an electric mixer until completely uniform.

Cream. To beat together a fat (typically butter or margarine) and a dry ingredient, like sugar, until soft and smooth. Electric mixers work best.

Fold. To incorporate a light, aerated mixture, such as egg whites, into a heavier batter without deflating the airy mixture. Incorporate egg whites with a rubber spatula, a third at a time, by using a gentle, folding motion. Scrape to the bottom of the bowl, then lift the spatula out and fold over the mixture. Repeat motion on the other side of the bowl until mixture is combined. Avoid brisk, stirring motions.

Mix. To blend a number of ingredients together by stirring or beating.

Separating Eggs. Break egg and catch yolk in one half of the shell. Let the white fall into a cup or small bowl. Continue by transferring yolk from one half of shell to the other until all the egg white has drained into bowl. Place yolk in a separate bowl.

Sift. To lighten and remove lumps from dry ingredients, such as flour and confectioners' sugar, by passing them through a flour sifter.

Whip. To incorporate air into an ingredient such as egg whites and cream so as to form stiff peaks.

FROSTING AND DECORATING TIPS

It's true. Frosting makes the cupcake, but *you* make the frosting. That's why we've included delicious, easy frosting recipes that will help you add this creamy layer of sweetness to your cupcakes and give them personality and festive appeal.

Some of our cupcakes—like our Pineapple Upside-Down Cupcakes, Perfect Picnic Cupcakes, or Tea Party Miniatures—don't need frosting. One of our cupcakes frosts itself! This children's favorite, Magic Self-

Frosting Cupcakes, adds an element of fun and surprise to the baking process.

There's no great secret to making frosting, but there are some basic tips that will help you get good results every time. For your convenience, all frosting recipes in this book have been included next to their cupcake recipes.

1. *Soften butter to room temperature.* Softened butter is easier to beat and blends better with other ingredients. Butter that is too soft, however, will not give you the creamy, spreading consistency you need for good frosting. Speed the softening process by slicing the chilled butter into a bowl, thereby increasing the amount of surface area exposed to warmer temperatures.

2. *If frosting is too thick,* add hot milk by the teaspoon until desired consistency, or set frosting in a metal bowl in a saucepan of simmering water. Beat until soft.

3. *If frosting is too thin,* add more sugar and beat until thick.

4. *Avoid certain frostings during hot humid weather;* glazes and whipped cream frostings aren't compatible with warm, humid days.

5. *Never frost cupcakes until they are completely cooled.* Save yourself the frustration and disappointment of icing warm cupcakes, unless the recipe directs otherwise. Cupcakes generally take about 1 hour to cool.

6. *Freeze leftover frosting*. Frosting freezes well in airtight containers. We sometimes double the recipe for certain frostings and freeze half for a future batch of cupcakes. Bring frozen frosting to room temperature and beat before use to revive fluffiness. Approximately 1 cup of frosting will amply cover 12 cupcakes.

When it comes to decorating cupcakes, we believe that simple is best. So we're leaving the fancy special effects to the trained pastry chefs and guiding you to decorating tips that are fast, easy, and surprisingly good looking.

Since kids love festive, colorfully decorated cupcakes, we've incorporated more of these ideas in the Cupcakes and Kids chapter.

1. *Keep it simple*. If the frosting is applied to a nicely risen cupcake and swirled in an appealing uniform fashion, most people will find it irresistible. A small sprinkling of chopped nuts, cake crumbs, or chocolate sprinkles is enough to give a cupcake a distinctive look.

2. *Avoid underfilling your pans with batter*. It takes a bit of practice to know how high to fill them, but I would say the general tendency is to underfill rather than overfill. The mistake of overfilled cupcake pans can be much more easily disguised with frosting than underfilled ones.

3. *Use small utensils to spread frosting*. Standard-size metal cake spatulas are difficult to work with on the small surfaces of cupcakes. Use

smaller spatulas. I use the knife from my children's cutlery set to spread frosting, and the back of a teaspoon to make decorative swirls.

4. *Stick to natural ingredients for coloring your frosting.* I prefer the natural colors of cherry juice, strawberries, and frozen orange juice concentrate, but there might be occasions when U.S.-certified food colors are more convenient or necessary in obtaining specific colors. The most commonly available food colorings are the liquid vegetable food colors available in grocery stores. I have found that to obtain rich colors with these requires using much more than the box directions suggest. Professional bakers' paste and powder colors, found in specialty cookware stores, generally give better results but are not as widely available.

   An easy alternative to using artificial colorings is to buy the packaged tubes of colored frosting available in the bakery section of grocery stores. These decorative frostings, made with vegetable shortening, make it convenient and easy to write, pipe borders, and create ornamental designs on your cupcakes.

5. *Use the dipping method whenever possible.* An alternative to spreading frosting with spatulas is the dipping method, which uses softer, thinner, boiled frostings. Simply dip the cupcake into the bowl of frosting and slowly twist it as you lift it from the bowl to form a peak. Kids love this method.

Cupcakes and Kids

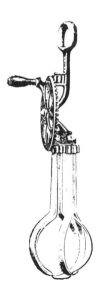

When I was a kid, I loved cupcakes. I enjoyed licking off the frosting and peeling back the paper wrapper with hopes of finding more frosting underneath. Then I grew up, pursued a career, and married Larry. For the longest time I forgot about cupcakes.

It wasn't until we thought about having our own children that cupcakes crept back into my consciousness. I would fantasize about my kids coming home from school to a big plate of homemade chocolate cupcakes waiting for them on the kitchen table. I'd pour them tall glasses of cold milk and they'd chatter with excitement about their school day as they licked the icing from their cupcakes and peeled back the paper wrappers.

After the children came along, my career seldom gave me the time I needed to live out those domestic fantasies. But as most families do, we've adapted and, fortunately, I've been lucky enough to merge my fantasy notion of cupcakes with my career. Hence, this cookbook and more cupcakes than any kid could ever imagine eating in his lifetime.

BAKING CUPCAKES WITH KIDS

We've discovered, as a family, that eating cupcakes is only half the fun. The anticipation of the finished product is enough to motivate any child to climb up on the kitchen stool and help out. I bought an old yellow enameled-metal stool at a yard sale for $2 that has paid for itself many times over in family fun. Now, whenever my young son, Henry, sees me in the kitchen getting the Mixmaster out, he enthusiastically starts sliding the yellow stool up to the counter and asks, "Can I help?"

Believe it or not there are a lot of basic skills for children of all ages to learn when baking. Numbers and math are applied when measuring ingredients, setting oven temperatures, and regulating the speeds on the electric mixer. Science is revealed through the chemistry of baking. Children love to conduct the baking-powder-freshness test (see page 12), mixing the baking powder with water to see if it fizzes. Motor skills and coordination are practiced when stirring, sifting, and cracking eggs. And creativity comes with the frosting and decorating of cupcakes. My son loves to squeeze the drops of food coloring from the tiny bottles to mix and blend colorful frostings. Overall, the process gives kids a sense of responsibility and helps build self-esteem. It's really great to see little ones grow and become more confident in the kitchen. We started including Henry when he was 2½ years old.

But what about the adults? Sometimes it can be a little nerve-racking to have kids "helping out" in the kitchen. Experience has taught us how to include kids in the baking process so that they feel helpful and good about the endeavor and we, the parents, aren't frazzled by the experience. Here are some tips to remember when baking cupcakes with kids.

1. *Safety first!* Assign designated work areas for children away from the oven or stove. Always supervise young children when operating electrical appliances. Restrict the use of knives, graters, and other sharp utensils.

2. *Wear aprons.* Aprons guard against spills and give kids (and grown-ups) a place to wipe their hands. We have a supply of fun aprons in a kitchen drawer that everyone feels free to use. Our favorites are some chef's aprons a friend sent us that read "Herman-Sombke

School of Cooking." Like a Little League team's uniform, it adds spirit to our family kitchen activities.

3. *Describe the ingredients.* When setting out the ingredients, say them out loud to your children to familiarize them with what goes into the recipe. This helps prepare them for what's to come.

4. *Keep the kids busy.* Try to occupy children with responsibilities they can accomplish on their own while you execute the stove-top or more difficult tasks. Children get bored if they have to wait around, so it's important to keep them occupied. Let them place the cupcake liners in the pan while you melt the chocolate squares in the saucepan, or have them sift flour as you separate eggs. Don't get frustrated if they want to leave the kitchen midway through the process. They'll be back to lick the spoons.

5. *Sifting flour is great fun for kids.* Crank-handled sifters are easier for little hands to use than squeeze-handled sifters. Prepare the area with waxed paper or paper towels to retrieve spilled flour.

6. *Let kids crack open the eggs.* This requires some patience, but children feel very rewarded once they've mastered it. (Our son successfully cracked his first egg into the bowl at age 2½. . . honest!) Be prepared for spills and make sure you have enough eggs on hand. Separating eggs requires skill and is probably better left for older children or adults.

7. *Liquids are easier for young children to pour than dry ingredients.* When

combining liquids and dry ingredients in a bowl, it's easier to let the kids pour the liquids. Generally I let my son operate the speeds on the Mixmaster and pour in the liquids, while I add the flour and sugar and scrape the sides of the bowl with the spatula.

8. *Use small spoons for ladling batter into cups.* I find there's less mess if you give kids teaspoons to transfer the batter into the cups. They can also use the backs of teaspoons to apply frosting.

9. *Involve children in the cleanup process.* Let them wash some of the utensils they were using or put them in the dishwasher. Small cleanup tasks give kids a sense of the entire baking process without detracting from the fun.

The following recipes are the ones we've found have the most appeal for kids, either for their decorative allure, flavor, or baking ease. We've been careful to include a few favorites for both girls and boys. The Tea Party Miniatures (page 50) look adorable on a child's tea service and make appropriate bite-size snacks. Boys love the baseball decoration and flavor of the Baseball Butterscotch Cupcake (page 46). Rainy Day Cupcakes (page 40) make for a good creative project and yummy treat when the weather keeps everyone indoors. And kids thrill to the soda fountain look and fresh root beer flavor of our Root Beer Float Cupcakes (page 48). We hope you have as much fun baking and eating these cupcakes with your kids as we have had with ours.

PEANUT BUTTER–FILLED CHOCOLATE CUPCAKES

Bite into these fudgy treats and discover the delicious peanut butter filling. No icing is necessary for these melt-in-your-mouth marvels.

PEANUT BUTTER FILLING
¼ cup creamy peanut butter

1 tablespoon light brown sugar

CAKE
3 squares (3 ounces) unsweetened chocolate, melted
2 cups sifted cake flour
1½ teaspoons baking powder
½ teaspoon baking soda
½ teaspoon salt

¼ pound butter, softened
1¼ cups firmly packed light brown sugar
1 teaspoon vanilla extract
2 eggs
1 cup milk

1. Position rack in center of oven; preheat to 350°F. Line two 12-cup muffin pans with paper cupcake liners. Make filling in a small bowl by stirring together peanut butter and brown sugar until well blended.

2. Using a double boiler, melt chocolate in top pan over hot water.

3. In a medium bowl, stir or whisk together flour, baking powder, baking soda, and salt.

4. In a large bowl and using an electric mixer, cream butter until soft and smooth. Gradually add sugar, creaming until fluffy. Add vanilla. Beat in eggs, one at a time, until thoroughly combined, then the chocolate.

5. Add dry ingredients alternately with milk, beating until smooth after each addition. Ladle half the cake batter into pans, filling cups halfway. Make a little well in the center of each batter-filled cup and spoon in a heaping ½ teaspoon of the filling. Cover with remaining cake batter.

6. Bake for 20 to 25 minutes, or until a toothpick inserted in center of one cupcake comes out clean. Remove pans from oven and place on wire racks for 5 minutes before turning cupcakes out onto racks. Reinvert immediately.

Yield: 24 cupcakes

• PINK PRINCESS CUPCAKES •

These delightful cupcakes are as delicately sweet and irresistibly charming as little girls. A swirl of whipped cream adorns fluffy pink strawberry frosting over downy white cake, all topped with a cherry. Good little girls deserve Pink Princess Cupcakes.

2 cups sifted cake flour
2 teaspoons baking powder
¼ teaspoon salt
¼ pound butter, softened

1⅓ cups granulated sugar
1½ teaspoons vanilla extract
⅔ cup milk
4 egg whites

1. Position rack in center of oven; preheat to 350°F. Line two 12-cup muffin pans with pink cupcake liners. (You can use the pink ones from a standard box of assorted colored liners.)

2. In a medium bowl, mix or whisk together flour, baking powder, and salt.

3. In a large bowl and using an electric mixer, cream butter until smooth and light. Gradually add 1 cup of the sugar, creaming until mixture is fluffy.

4. Mix vanilla with milk. Add dry ingredients alternately with milk, beating until smooth after each addition.

5. Using clean beaters and a separate bowl, beat egg whites until stiff, then gradually beat in remaining ⅓ cup sugar. Fold mixture thoroughly into cake batter. Ladle batter into pans, filling cups two-thirds full. Bake 20 minutes, or until a cake tester inserted in center of one cupcake comes

out clean and cake springs back when pressed lightly in center. Remove pans from oven and place on wire racks for 5 minutes before turning cupcakes out onto wire racks. Reinvert immediately.

STRAWBERRY CREAM FROSTING
4 tablespoons butter
2 cups confectioners' sugar
1¼ teaspoons vanilla extract

1 teaspoon lemon juice
⅓ cup fresh puréed strawberries

WHIPPED CREAM TOPPING
¾ cup heavy cream
2 tablespoons confectioners' sugar

9 maraschino cherries, halved

1. In medium bowl and using an electric mixer, cream butter until soft. Gradually add 1 cup of the sugar, creaming until fluffy. Beat in vanilla. Add lemon juice, then remaining sugar alternately with strawberry purée, beating after each addition until smooth. (For a pinker color, add a few drops of red food coloring.) Set aside.

2. Beat cream in a separate bowl, adding sugar as cream begins to thicken. Place in refrigerator until ready to use. Generously frost cupcakes with strawberry frosting. Place a dollop of whipped cream in center of each cupcake, swirling to a peak. Top with maraschino cherry.

Yield: 18 cupcakes

• KIT-KAT CUPCAKES •

We developed this cupcake for our young daughter, Kit, whom we endearingly call Kit Kat. This is an easy chocolate cake recipe for kids to make. Everything is mixed in one bowl and the topping is chunks of the popular crisp chocolate wafer candy bar. They're scrumptious!

3 (4-ounce) Kit-Kat bars
2 cups sifted cake flour
1½ teaspoons baking powder
½ teaspoon baking soda
¼ teaspoon salt
½ cup plus 3 tablespoons cocoa
1½ cups granulated sugar

¼ pound plus 3 tablespoons butter,
  softened
½ cup warm water
⅔ cup milk
2 eggs
1½ teaspoons vanilla extract

1. Position rack in center of oven; preheat to 350°F. Line two 12-cup muffin pans with paper cupcake liners.

2. Using a food processor or blender, pulverize 1 of the Kit Kat bars into fine crumbs. (Do not leave any large pieces.) Using a knife, chop remaining bars into ¼-inch cubes for frosting. Set aside.

3. In a large bowl and using an electric mixer, stir or whisk together the sifted flour, baking powder, baking soda, salt, cocoa, and sugar.

4. Add the butter, water, milk, eggs, and vanilla and blend on low speed until ingredients are moist. On medium speed, mix for 3 minutes, scraping frequently to blend all ingredients completely. Scrape down sides of bowl. Fold in finely ground Kit Kat crumbs until well blended.

5. Ladle batter into pans, filling cups two-thirds full. Bake 25 to 30 minutes, or until a cake tester inserted in center of one cupcake comes out clean and cake springs back when pressed lightly in center. Remove pans from oven and place on wire racks for 5 minutes before turning cupcakes out onto racks. Reinvert immediately. When thoroughly cool, frost with Chocolate Kit Kat Frosting.

CHOCOLATE KIT KAT FROSTING

4 tablespoons butter, softened	1 teaspoon vanilla extract
2 cups sifted confectioners' sugar	1 to 2 tablespoons milk
½ cup cocoa	Cubed Kit Kat bars

Using an electric mixer, cream butter until smooth. Stir together sugar and cocoa and gradually add to butter, creaming until smooth. Add vanilla. If frosting is too thick, add milk to desired spreading consistency. Stir in cubed Kit Kat bars until mixed consistently through frosting. Frost cupcakes when cool.

Yield: 18 cupcakes

◆ MAGIC SELF-FROSTING CUPCAKES ◆

These cupcakes frost themselves! Kids love the thrill of discovering the chocolate frosting on top of the cupcakes when they're inverted from the pan.

2 squares (2 ounces) unsweetened chocolate
1 can condensed milk
6 tablespoons butter, softened
1 cup granulated sugar
2 eggs, well beaten

1 teaspoon vanilla extract
1½ cups sifted cake flour
1¾ teaspoons baking powder
¼ teaspoon salt
½ cup milk

1. Position rack in center of oven; preheat to 350°F. Grease and flour a 12-cup muffin pan.

2. Using a double boiler, melt chocolate in top pan over hot water, stirring frequently. Remove chocolate pan from over hot water. Add condensed milk and mix well. Pour approximately 1 tablespoon of chocolate mixture into bottom of each bake cup. Set aside.

3. In a large bowl and using an electric mixer, cream butter until smooth and light. Gradually add sugar, beating until mixture is fluffy. Add beaten eggs and vanilla and beat well.

4. In a medium bowl, stir together sifted flour, baking powder, and salt. Stir in dry ingredients alternately with milk, beginning and ending with dry ingredients, and blending well after each addition. Scrape down

sides of bowl. Pour batter over cooled chocolate mixture in muffin pans, filling cups two-thirds full.

5. Bake 25 minutes, or until a cake tester inserted in center of one cupcake comes out clean and cake springs back when pressed lightly in center. Remove pan from oven and place on wire rack for 5 minutes before turning cupcakes out onto racks. The chocolate will be on the top.

Yield: 12 cupcakes

· ICE CREAM SUNDAE CUPCAKES ·

These make fun birthday party desserts and can be prepared ahead to save the fuss and muss of scooping out ice cream at the party.

¾ cup unsweetened cocoa
¾ cup boiling water
2 cups sifted cake flour
2 teaspoons baking powder
½ teaspoon baking soda
½ teaspoon salt

¼ pound plus 2 tablespoons butter,
  softened
1½ cups granulated sugar
2 eggs
2 teaspoons vanilla extract
½ cup milk

ICE CREAM AND TOPPING
½ gallon vanilla ice cream
1 can Hershey's Chocolate Syrup
1 can commercial whipped cream

16 maraschino cherries
Chopped nuts

1. Position rack in center of oven; preheat to 350°F. Line two 12-cup muffin pans with paper cupcake liners.

2. In a small bowl, dissolve cocoa in boiling water until creamy, then let cool to room temperature. In a medium bowl, stir or whisk together flour, baking powder, baking soda, and salt.

3. In a large bowl and using an electric mixer, beat butter until smooth and creamy. Gradually add sugar, creaming mixture until very fluffy. Beat in eggs one at a time until blended. Gradually add dry ingredients until moistened, beating 1½ minutes.

4. Combine vanilla, milk, and cooled cocoa mixture. Gradually blend into flour mixture and beat for 1½ minutes. Pour batter into pans, filling each cup two-thirds full.

5. Bake 20 to 25 minutes, or until a cake tester inserted in center of one cupcake comes out clean and cake springs back when pressed lightly in center. Remove pans from oven and place on wire racks for 5 minutes before turning cupcakes out onto racks. Reinvert immediately.

6. When cupcakes are completely cool, use a tablespoon to scoop out cake from the top of each cupcake, enough to form a well for a scoop of vanilla ice cream. (Freeze scoops of cake in an airtight plastic bag to use as toppings for other cupcakes.) Using an ice cream scoop, place a scoop of vanilla ice cream in the well of each cupcake.* Top with chocolate syrup, whipped cream, a sprinkling of nuts, and maraschino cherry.

Yield: 16 cupcakes

---

*To save time in serving, ice cream can be placed on cupcakes, covered with plastic wrap, and frozen. Remove from freezer 15 minutes before serving and cover with toppings.

• RAINY DAY CUPCAKES •

These are as much fun to make as they are to eat. The one-bowl cake batter method makes it an easy recipe for kids. A friend baked the cupcakes ahead and saved the decorating part as a fun "create your own cupcake" activity at her 6-year-old's birthday party. The trick is to set out as many cake toppings as possible and let the kids be creative.

¼ pound butter, softened
1 cup granulated sugar
3 eggs (separate white from 1 egg
* and reserve for frosting)*
2 cups sifted cake flour

2¼ teaspoons baking powder
¼ teaspoon salt
½ cup milk
1 teaspoon vanilla extract

1. Position rack in center of oven; preheat to 350°F. Line two 12-cup muffin pans with paper cupcake liners.

2. In a large bowl and using an electric mixer, cream butter until smooth. Gradually add sugar until mixture is smooth and fluffy. Beat in eggs until well blended.

3. Stir in flour, baking powder, and salt until moistened.

4. Mix milk and vanilla together and gradually add to flour mixture, beating until smooth. Pour batter into pans, filling each cup about two-thirds full.

5. Bake 20 to 25 minutes, or until a cake tester inserted in center of one cupcake comes out clean and cake springs back when pressed lightly in center. Remove pans from oven and place on wire racks for 5 minutes before turning cupcakes out onto racks. Reinvert immediately. Prepare frosting.

Rainy Day Frosting

1 egg white (reserved from cake
  batter)
1 cup granulated sugar

¼ teaspoon cream of tartar
½ cup boiling water

Topping Suggestions

M & M's
Sprinkles
Cereal
Tubes of colored cake decorating
  frosting (kids really love using
  these)
Chopped nuts

Raisins
Shredded coconut
Gumdrops
Chocolate chips
(Use your imagination, the more
  topping selections the better.)

1. In a medium mixing bowl, combine egg white, sugar, and cream of tartar.

2. Have boiling water ready and start mixer at low speed. Gradually pour in boiling water and increase speed. Mix about 7 minutes, until frosting is proper consistency for spreading.

3. When cupcakes are completely cooled, spread with frosting. Use fluted bake cups to pour toppings into and place them in the center of the table within children's reach. Let children decorate their own cupcakes. When they're finished, it's fun to place them all together in the center of the table and take a picture of the results.

Yield: 18 cupcakes

· ICE CREAM CONE CUPCAKES ·

This recipe uses a technique that kids love. The batter is poured into flat-bottomed ice cream cones and baked. The cake is then frosted and kids lick and eat them as if they were eating ice cream cones.

12 flat-bottomed ice cream cones
1¾ cups sifted cake flour
2 teaspoons baking powder
¼ teaspoon salt
2 eggs, separated

¼ pound butter, softened
1 cup granulated sugar
1½ teaspoons vanilla extract
½ cup milk

1. Position rack in center of oven; preheat to 350°F. Arrange 12 ice cream cones on a baking sheet.

2. In a medium bowl, stir or whisk together flour, baking powder, and salt.

3. In a separate bowl, beat the egg yolks.

4. In a large bowl and using an electric mixer, cream butter until soft and smooth. Gradually add sugar, creaming until fluffy. Add vanilla and beat in well-beaten egg yolks. Add flour alternately with milk, beating until smooth after each addition.

5. In a separate bowl, beat egg whites until stiff but not dry and fold into batter until thoroughly combined. Pour into ice cream cones, filling each cone two-thirds full.

6. Bake 20 to 25 minutes, or until a cake tester inserted in center of one cupcake comes out clean and cake springs back when pressed lightly in

center. Remove baking sheet from oven and place cones on a wire rack until completely cooled. Prepare frosting.

CREAMY CHOCOLATE FROSTING

2 squares (2 ounces) unsweetened
chocolate
½ cup milk
1½ cups granulated sugar

2 egg yolks, well beaten
1 tablespoon butter
1 teaspoon vanilla extract

1. In a saucepan, heat chocolate and milk over low heat until chocolate is melted. Using a hand-held electric mixer, beat until smooth.

2. In a small bowl, gradually stir sugar into egg yolks. Pour into saucepan of chocolate milk mixture, stirring frequently and cooking over low heat for 8 to 10 minutes, or until thick. Stir in butter until melted. Stir in vanilla and remove from heat. When lukewarm, beat until thick enough to spread. Frost ice cream cones and decorate with rainbow sprinkles.

Yield: 12 cupcakes

• PERFECT PICNIC CUPCAKES •

Frosting generally makes cupcakes sticky subjects to pack for picnics. But these moist orange-flavored cupcakes with creamy coconut centers make perfect picnic basket companions on hot summer days.

COCONUT CREAM CHEESE FILLING

4 ounces cream cheese	*1 egg*
⅓ cup granulated sugar	*½ cup coconut*

ORANGE CAKE

2¼ cups sifted cake flour	*1½ cups granulated sugar*
3 teaspoons baking powder	*3 eggs, separated*
½ teaspoon salt	*½ cup cold water*
¼ pound plus 4 tablespoons butter,	*½ cup orange juice*
* softened*	*2 tablespoons orange zest*

1. Position rack in center of oven; preheat to 350°F. Line two 12-cup muffin pans with paper cupcake liners.

2. Prepare filling in a small bowl using an electric mixer. Beat cream cheese and sugar, gradually adding egg and beating until fluffy. Stir in coconut until well blended. Set aside.

3. In a medium bowl, mix or whisk together flour, baking powder, and salt.

4. In a large bowl and using an electric mixer, cream butter until smooth

and light. Gradually add 1 cup of the sugar, creaming until mixture is fluffy.

5. In a small bowl, beat egg whites with electric mixer until foamy. Gradually add the remaining ½ cup sugar and continue beating until the whites are stiff but not dry. Set aside.

6. In a medium bowl, combine egg yolks, water, and orange juice. Beat on medium speed until mixture is thick. Add to butter and sugar mixture, mixing gently until blended. Mix in dry ingredients until moist. Gently fold in egg whites until mixture is well combined. Ladle batter into lined muffin pans. Sprinkle tops of cupcakes with orange zest.

7. Bake 20 to 25 minutes, or until a cake tester inserted in center of one cupcake comes out clean and cake springs back when pressed lightly in center. Remove pans from oven and place on wire racks for 5 minutes before turning cupcakes out onto racks. Reinvert immediately to prevent cakes from sticking to racks.

Yield: 18 cupcakes

• BASEBALL BUTTERSCOTCH CUPCAKES •

The baseball decoration on these cupcakes scores a home run with boys and is a big hit at birthday or Little League parties. Leave the baseball motif off the frosting and the delicious butterscotch flavor is a favorite with either gender.

CAKE

1⅓ cups sifted cake flour
¾ cup firmly packed light brown sugar
1¾ teaspoons baking powder
¼ teaspoon salt

4 tablespoons butter, softened
⅔ cup milk
1 egg
1 teaspoon vanilla extract
6 ounces butterscotch bits

1. Position rack in center of oven; preheat to 350°F. Line a 12-cup miniature muffin pan with paper cupcake liners.

2. In a large mixing bowl, stir or whisk together flour, sugar, baking powder, and salt.

3. Add butter and milk, beating on low speed 1½ minutes. Add egg and vanilla and beat on low speed an additional 1½ minutes. Fold in butterscotch bits. Ladle batter into muffin pan, filling each cup three-quarters full.

4. Bake 20 to 25 minutes, or until a cake tester inserted in center of one cupcake comes out clean and cake springs back when pressed lightly in center. Remove pan from oven and place on a wire rack for 5 minutes before turning cupcakes out onto racks. Reinvert immediately.

BUTTERSCOTCH FROSTING

¼ pound butter, softened
½ cup white vegetable shortening
2 teaspoons maple syrup
3½ to 4 cups sifted confectioners'
   sugar

2 to 3 tablespoons milk
1 small tube each of red and
   chocolate cake decorating frosting

1. Using an electric mixer, cream butter and shortening until smooth and completely blended. Add the maple syrup. With mixer on low speed, gradually mix in 3½ cups of the sugar, scraping sides of bowl.

2. Add the milk and beat frosting on high speed. If frosting is too thin, add more sugar. If it gets too thick, add more milk. Beat until light and fluffy.

3. Frost each cupcake with a generous layer of frosting. Smooth surface flat with a spatula to prepare for applying baseball decoration. Use chocolate frosting to make curved seams of baseball. Use red to make seam stitches.

Yield: 12 cupcakes

• ROOT BEER FLOAT CUPCAKES •

The root beer flavor is in the frosting of this soda fountain-style cupcake.

2 cups sifted cake flour	*1⅓ cups granulated sugar*
2 teaspoons baking powder	*1½ teaspoons vanilla extract*
¼ teaspoon salt	*⅔ cup milk*
¼ pound butter, softened	*4 egg whites*

1. Position rack in center of oven; preheat to 350°F. Line two 12-cup muffin pans with paper cupcake liners.

2. In a medium bowl, mix or whisk together flour, baking powder, and salt.

3. In a large bowl and using an electric mixer, cream butter until smooth and light. Gradually add 1 cup of the sugar, creaming until mixture is fluffy. Stir in vanilla.

4. Add dry ingredients alternately with milk, beating until smooth after each addition.

5. Beat egg whites until stiff, gradually beating in remaining ⅓ cup sugar. Fold mixture thoroughly into cake batter.

6. Pour batter into pans, filling each cup about two-thirds full. Bake 25 minutes, or until a cake tester inserted in center of one cupcake comes out clean and cake springs back when pressed lightly in center. Remove pans from oven and place on wire racks for 5 minutes before turning cupcakes out onto racks. Reinvert immediately. Frost when cupcakes are cool.

ROOT BEER FLOAT FROSTING

2 egg whites
1½ cups granulated sugar
⅓ cup old-fashioned root beer
2 teaspoons light corn syrup

¼ teaspoon cream of tartar
9 to 10 old-fashioned root beer
    candy sticks, or 18 colorful
    drinking straws.

1. In top pan of double boiler, combine all ingredients and beat with a hand-held electric mixer over boiling water. Begin at medium speed for 4 minutes and increase to high for 3 minutes. Whip icing until it holds soft peaks.

2. Remove pan from heat and beat on high for 1 full minute, or until frosting is thick enough for spreading. Spread on cooled cupcakes, swirling frosting with back of a spoon up to a single peak (to resemble a soft-serve ice cream cone).

3. Break root beer candy sticks in half and insert broken end into cupcake to resemble a drinking straw in a root beer float. Or substitute real drinking straws cut in half.

Yield: 18 cupcakes

• TEA PARTY MINIATURES •

These dainty little almond-flavored cakes are adorable when served on a child's tea service, and great when the kids play house. They make ideal portions for toddlers and can be easily frozen and thawed for spontaneous consumption. Caution: Adults are easily addicted to these tiny temptations.

1 cup sugar
¼ pound plus 4 tablespoons butter, softened
3 eggs
1¼ teaspoons almond extract
1 teaspoon vanilla extract

⅔ cup sour cream
2 cups sifted cake flour
½ teaspoon baking powder
½ teaspoon baking soda
¼ teaspoon salt

1. Position rack in center of oven; preheat to 350°F. Line two 12-cup miniature muffin pans with paper cupcake liners.

2. In a large mixing bowl, combine sugar, butter, and eggs and beat well. Mix in almond and vanilla extracts and sour cream.

3. In a medium mixing bowl, stir or whisk together flour, baking powder, baking soda, and salt. With mixer on medium speed, gradually add flour to egg mixture in three batches, beating for 20 seconds after each addition. Scrape down sides of bowl and place 2 teaspoons of batter into each prepared muffin cup.

4. Bake 15 minutes, or until a cake tester inserted in center of one cupcake comes out clean and cake springs back when pressed lightly in

center. Be careful not to overbake. Remove pans from oven and place on wire racks for 10 minutes before turning cupcakes out onto racks. Reinvert immediately to prevent cakes from sticking to racks.

5. When completely cooled, use a sifter to dust each cake with powdered sugar.

Yield: 24 cupcakes

• HENRY'S RACE CAR CUPCAKES •

These are the cupcakes we made for our son's fifth birthday pre-school party. Each cake has a chocolate candy kiss in the center, and is decorated with chocolate frosting and a miniature race car, which becomes the party favor. It was a thrill for Henry to help make them because he got to unwrap all the candy kisses and put them in each cup of batter, and later put a toy race car on top. To transport the cupcakes, we bought a cake box from our local bakery and let Henry color the outside with a race track and then glue some cars to the raceway. He still talks about these cupcakes.

2 cups sifted cake flour
2 teaspoons baking powder
¼ teaspoon salt
¼ pound butter, softened
1 cup granulated sugar

2 teaspoons vanilla extract
2 eggs, separated
⅔ cup milk
24 chocolate kiss candies

1. Position rack in center of oven; preheat to 375° F. Line two 12-cup muffin pans with paper cupcake liners.

2. In a medium bowl, stir or whisk together flour, baking powder, and salt.

3. In a large bowl and using an electric mixer, cream butter until soft and smooth. Gradually add sugar, creaming until fluffy. Add vanilla. In a small bowl, beat egg yolks until thick and beat into butter mixture. Add flour mixture alternately with milk, beating until smooth after each addition.

4. Beat egg whites until stiff and fold into batter until thoroughly com-

bined. Ladle half the batter into pans, filling each cup one-third full. Stick a candy kiss gently down into batter in each cup. Cover with batter until cup is two-thirds full.

5. Bake 20 to 25 minutes, or until a cake tester inserted in center of one cupcake comes out clean and cake springs back when pressed lightly in center. Remove pans from oven and place on wire racks for 10 minutes before turning cupcakes out onto racks. Reinvert immediately.

CHOCOLATE CREAM FROSTING

4 squares (4 ounces) unsweetened
    chocolate
½ cup cream
1½ cups sifted confectioners' sugar
2 egg yolks, well beaten
2 tablespoons butter
1 teaspoon vanilla extract

24 miniature toy cars (these can be
    purchased inexpensively in
    supermarket toy sections or toy
    stores)

1. Combine chocolate and cream in top pan of a double boiler over hot water. Cook, stirring constantly, until chocolate melts and mixture is smooth and blended. Add 1 cup of the sugar to chocolate mixture and cook until smooth.

2. Beat egg yolks with remaining sugar and stir into mixture. Add butter and cook 2 minutes longer. Add vanilla. Using a hand-held electric mixer, beat until thick and creamy. Cool and frost cupcakes. Place a toy car on top of each cupcake.

Yield: 24 cupcakes

• CHOCOLATE MARSHMALLOW CUPCAKES •

Creamy marshmallow frosting on dreamy chocolate cake make these a standard favorite among kids.

*3 squares (3 ounces) unsweetened
    chocolate*
2 cups sifted cake flour
2½ teaspoons baking powder
¼ teaspoon salt
¼ pound butter, softened

1 cup granulated sugar
2 egg whites
3 egg yolks
1 cup milk
1 teaspoon vanilla extract

1. Position rack in center of oven; preheat to 350° F. Line two 12-cup muffin pans with paper cupcake liners.

2. Using a double boiler, melt chocolate in top pan over hot water. Remove chocolate pan from over water. In a medium bowl, stir or whisk together flour, baking powder, and salt.

3. In a large bowl and using an electric mixer, cream butter until soft and smooth. Gradually add ½ cup of the sugar, creaming until fluffy. Blend in chocolate. Set aside.

4. In a separate bowl and using clean beaters, beat egg whites and remaining ½ cup sugar until stiff and set aside.

5. Beat egg yolks until thick and lemon colored and add to butter and sugar mixture. Add flour alternately with milk, beating until smooth after each addition. Add vanilla.

6. Fold beaten egg whites into batter until thoroughly combined. Ladle batter into pans, filling each cup two-thirds full.

7. Bake 20 minutes, or until a cake tester inserted in center of one cupcake comes out clean and cake springs back when pressed lightly in center. Remove pans from oven and place on wire racks for 10 minutes before turning cupcakes out onto racks. Reinvert immediately.

CREAMY MARSHMALLOW FROSTING

12 marshmallows
1½ cups granulated sugar
½ cup water

½ tablespoon light corn syrup
2 eggs whites
1 teaspoon vanilla extract

1. Cut marshmallows into small cubes and set aside.

2. In a saucepan, combine sugar, water, and corn syrup, stirring over low heat until sugar dissolves. Cover and boil about 3 minutes, then boil uncovered without stirring until a small amount of syrup forms a soft ball when dropped into cold water (or reaches 238° F on a candy thermometer). Remove syrup from heat and gently stir in marshmallows until melted.

3. In a small mixing bowl and using an electric mixer, quickly beat egg whites until stiff.

4. With mixer on medium speed, pour marshmallow syrup in a very fine stream over egg whites, beating constantly. Add vanilla and continue beating until frosting is cool and forms soft peaks. Use a tablespoon to spoon frosting onto cupcakes, swirling in an upward motion to form a peak.

Yield: 18 cupcakes

• EASY CARROT CUPCAKES •

This recipe is both delicious and nutritious, and easy for kids to make. There's no electric mixer required—everything is hand-mixed in one bowl.

2 cups all-purpose flour
2 teaspoons baking powder
2 teaspoons baking soda
2 teaspoons cinnamon
½ teaspoon salt
1 cup granulated sugar
⅔ cup firmly packed light brown sugar

1 cup vegetable oil
3 eggs
3 cups grated carrot
2 teaspoons grated orange rind
½ cup chopped walnuts
⅔ cup raisins

1. Position rack in center of oven; preheat to 325° F. Line two 12-cup muffin pans with paper cupcake liners.

2. In a large mixing bowl, stir together the flour, baking powder, baking soda, cinnamon, and salt. In a medium bowl, beat together the granulated and brown sugar, oil, and eggs. Pour the mixture into the dry ingredients, stirring until blended.

3. In a medium bowl, stir together carrot, orange rind, nuts, and raisins. Fold into batter until well blended. Ladle into prepared pans, filling each cup two-thirds full.

4. Bake 25 minutes, or until a cake tester inserted in center of one cupcake comes out clean and cake springs back when pressed lightly in

center. Remove pans from oven and place on wire racks. When cupcakes are completely cooled, remove from pan and frost.

EASY CREAM CHEESE FROSTING

6 ounces cream cheese, softened
2 tablespoons butter, softened
2 teaspoons vanilla extract

3½ to 4 cups sifted confectioners' sugar
1 to 2 tablespoons milk, as needed

In a small mixing bowl and using an electric mixer, cream together cream cheese, butter, and vanilla. Gradually add sugar, beating until fluffy. If frosting is too thick, add milk as needed to create desired spreading consistency. Spread on thoroughly cool cupcakes.

Yield: 18 cupcakes

• SCHOOL PARTY CUPCAKES •

The first time we ever baked cupcakes for a party at our son's preschool, it was suggested that we send at least 24 cupcakes. No problem, we thought. In typical fashion, we baked them late at night after a very hectic day, and to our dismay the recipe yielded only 20 cupcakes. In a panic we whipped up another batch. To save you from this same dilemma, we've devised this easy crowd-pleasing recipe that guarantees a yield of at least 24 cupcakes. The result is two superbly flavored cakes—vanilla and chocolate—and two frostings—buttercream and chocolate buttercream—to mix and match on the cakes as you please.

3 squares (3 ounces) semisweet chocolate	½ pound butter, softened
4 cups sifted cake flour	2 cups granulated sugar
2 tablespoons baking powder	4 eggs
1 teaspoon salt	1 tablespoon vanilla extract
	1⅓ cups milk

1. Position racks to divide oven in thirds; preheat to 350°F. Line two 12-cup muffin pans with paper cupcake liners.

2. Using a double boiler, melt chocolate in top pan over hot water, stirring frequently. Remove chocolate pan from over hot water.

3. In a medium bowl, stir together flour, baking powder, and salt.

4. In a large bowl and using an electric mixer, cream butter until smooth and light. Gradually add sugar, beating until mixture is light and fluffy.

Add eggs, one at a time, beating for 20 seconds after each addition until mixture is light and well blended. Stir in vanilla extract.

5. Stir in dry ingredients alternately with milk, beginning and ending with dry ingredients, blending well after each addition. Scrape down sides of bowl and remove half the batter to another medium bowl. Stir the melted chocolate into one of the bowls of batter until uniform in color. Ladle yellow batter into one pan and chocolate batter into the other, filling each cup about two-thirds full.

6. Bake 20 minutes, or until a cake tester inserted in center of one cupcake comes out clean and cake springs back when pressed lightly in center. Remove pans from oven and place on wire racks for 10 minutes before turning cupcakes out onto racks. Reinvert immediately to prevent cakes from sticking to racks. Cool thoroughly and frost half with Chocolate Buttercream Frosting and the other half with Vanilla Butter Cream Frosting.

CHOCOLATE AND VANILLA BUTTERCREAM FROSTING

3 squares (3 ounces) semisweet
    chocolate
1/4 pound plus 4 tablespoons butter,
    softened
1 egg yolk
1/4 teaspoon salt

2 teaspoons vanilla extract
6 to 6 1/2 cups sifted confectioners'
    sugar
7 or 8 tablespoons heavy cream or
    milk, or as needed

1. Using a double boiler, melt chocolate in top pan over hot water, stirring frequently. Remove chocolate pan from over hot water.

2. In a medium bowl and using an electric mixer, cream butter until soft, then beat in egg yolk, salt, and vanilla. Mixing at low speed, add ½ cup of the sugar, beating until smooth. Remove half the mixture to a separate medium bowl. In one mixture, beat in melted chocolate and alternately add 3 to 4 tablespoons cream and 2 cups of the sugar until smooth. Scrape down sides of bowl. If frosting is too thin, add more sugar; if too stiff, add more cream.

3. In remaining bowl of butter, egg, and sugar mixture, beat in 3 to 4 tablespoons cream and 2 cups sugar, blending smooth between additions. Scrape down sides of bowl. Add more sugar if too thin; more cream if too stiff.

4. Generously frost half the cupcakes with the vanilla buttercream frosting and the other half with the chocolate. Decorate vanilla frosted cupcakes with chocolate sprinkles and the chocolate frosted cupcakes with white sprinkles. (Rainbow sprinkles, M & M's, and other colorful candy may also be used, but we prefer the uniform look of chocolate and vanilla.)

Yield: 24 cupcakes

Dinner Party
Cupcakes

Some people associate cupcakes only with children's parties or casual buffets; however, cupcakes can make elegant dinner party desserts. Served to guests on individual cake plates, their inherent single portions provide the perfect amount of cake after a large meal.

Most of these cupcakes are adaptations of classic cake recipes.

• GINGERBREAD CUPCAKES •

These are light and moist, and taste good warm or cooled with a whipped cream topping.

4 tablespoon butter, softened	*1½ cups all-purpose flour*
½ cup granulated sugar	*1 teaspoon baking soda*
1 egg	*1 teaspoon cinnamon*
½ cup molasses	*1½ teaspoons ground ginger*
¾ cup boiling water	*¼ teaspoon salt*

1. Position rack in center of oven; preheat to 325°F. Line a 12-cup muffin pan with paper cupcake liners.

2. In a large mixing bowl and using an electric mixer, cream butter until soft, then gradually add sugar, beating until fluffy and light. Beat in egg until combined, then blend in molasses and boiling water.

3. In a medium bowl, sift together flour, baking soda, cinnamon, ginger, and salt. With mixer on low speed, slowly pour dry ingredients into sugar mixture, beating until smooth. Ladle into pans, filling each cup two-thirds full.

4. Bake 30 to 35 minutes, or until a cake tester inserted in center of one cupcake comes out clean and cake springs back when pressed lightly in center. Remove pan from oven and place on wire rack for 5 minutes before turning cupcakes out onto rack. Reinvert immediately. Serve warm with whipped cream or allow to cool and dust with confectioners' sugar.

Yield: 12 cupcakes

• MARBLE CUPCAKES •

Individual portions of contrasting yellow and chocolate cake with creamy chocolate frosting make these cupcakes a sweet temptation at any social gathering.

10²⁄₃ tablespoons butter, softened
2¼ cups granulated sugar
4 eggs
2 teaspoons vanilla extract
3 cups sifted cake flour
1¼ teaspoons baking powder

1 teaspoon baking soda
½ teaspoon salt
1²⁄₃ cups buttermilk
½ cup unsweetened cocoa
¼ cup water

1. Position rack in center of oven; preheat to 350° F. Line two 12-cup muffin pans with paper cupcake liners.

2. In a large mixing bowl and using an electric mixer, cream butter, gradually beating in 2 cups of the sugar, until light and fluffy. Beat in eggs until well blended, then mix in vanilla.

3. In a medium bowl, stir or whisk together flour, baking powder, ¾ teaspoon of the baking soda, and salt. Add dry ingredients alternately with buttermilk to butter mixture, beating on medium speed until batter is smooth.

4. In a small bowl, stir together the cocoa, remaining ¼ cup sugar, and remaining ¼ teaspoon baking soda. Add water and blend until smooth. Remove 1½ cups of yellow batter and blend into chocolate mixture. With yellow batter, fill each cup of pan one-third full, then spoon 1 tablespoon

of chocolate batter on top. Cover with yellow batter until two-thirds full. Using a butter knife, draw it once through each cup of batter, for a gentle marbled effect. (With cupcakes, be careful not to overblend batters or you will lose the marbleized effect.)

5. Bake 30 minutes, or until a cake tester inserted in center of one cupcake comes out clean and cake springs back when pressed lightly in center. Remove pans from oven and place on wire racks for 10 minutes before turning cupcakes out onto racks. Reinvert immediately. Frost with Chocolate Cream Frosting.

CHOCOLATE CREAM FROSTING

4 squares (4 ounces) unsweetened chocolate
½ cup cream
1½ cups sifted confectioners' sugar

2 egg yolks, well beaten
2 tablespoons butter
1 teaspoon vanilla extract

1. Combine chocolate and cream in top pan of a double boiler over hot water. Heat, stirring constantly, until chocolate melts and mixture is smooth and blended. Add 1 cup of the sugar to chocolate mixture and cook until smooth.

2. Beat egg yolks with remaining ½ cup sugar and stir into mixture. Add butter and cook 2 minutes longer. Add vanilla. Using a hand-held electric mixer, beat until thick and creamy. Let mixture cool before frosting cupcakes.

Yield: 18 cupcakes

• BLACK FOREST CUPCAKES •

These miniature renditions of the Viennese torte taste as good as they look . . . and they're easy to make.

2 squares (2 ounces) unsweetened chocolate	3 eggs
¼ pound butter, softened	1 teaspoon vanilla extract
1 cup granulated sugar	2 cups sifted cake flour
½ cup firmly packed light brown sugar	1 teaspoon baking soda
	¼ teaspoon salt
	1 cup buttermilk

1. Position rack in center of oven; preheat to 350°F. Line two 12-cup muffin pans with paper cupcake liners.

2. Melt chocolate in top pan of a double boiler over hot water. Let cool. In a large mixing bowl and using an electric mixer, cream butter. Gradually add granulated and brown sugar, beating until light and fluffy. Add the eggs one at a time, beating well after each addition. Add vanilla. Blend in chocolate.

3. In a medium bowl, stir or whisk together flour, baking soda, and salt. With mixer on low speed, add the flour and buttermilk alternately to batter, beginning and ending with flour. Ladle mixture into pans, filling each cup two-thirds full.

4. Bake 20 to 25 minutes, or until a cake tester inserted in center of one cupcake comes out clean and cake springs back when pressed lightly in center. Remove pans from oven and place on wire racks for 10 minutes

before turning cupcakes out onto racks. Reinvert immediately. Cool completely.

TOPPING

1 cup canned tart cherries (at least 18 cherries)	*2 teaspoons kirsh (optional)*
	½ cup cherry preserves
1 (8-ounce) bar of dark chocolate, at room temperature	*2 cups heavy cream*
	2 tablespoons sugar

1. Drain canned cherries completely, patting excess juice with paper towels. (If not totally drained, juice will bleed onto whipped cream topping.)

2. Make shaved chocolate curls with a vegetable peeler, working at the end of the chocolate bar to create narrow shavings. Shave onto a piece of waxed paper and store in refrigerator until ready to use.

3. If you are including the kirsh to flavor the cherry preserves, stir kirsh into preserves a teaspoon at a time for desired taste. The liqueur should not overwhelm the flavor of the preserves. Using a small spatula or butter knife, spread a thin layer of preserves over each cupcake.

4. In a medium bowl, whip cream with sugar until stiff peaks form. With a tablespoon, put a generous dollop of whipped cream on each cake, using the back of the spoon to swirl the cream into a peak. Sprinkle chocolate shavings over cream and top each cake with a cherry. Refrigerate cupcakes until 15 to 20 minutes before serving.

Yield: 18 cupcakes

• PINEAPPLE UPSIDE-DOWN CUPCAKES •

This is one of our all-time favorite cupcakes. These little upside-down cakes will totally dazzle your guests.

PINEAPPLE TOPPING
5 tablespoons butter
½ cup firmly packed light brown sugar
6 slices canned pineapple, drained
12 maraschino cherry halves, drained

CAKE
1⅓ cups sifted all-purpose flour
1 cup granulated sugar
2 teaspoons baking powder
½ teaspoon salt
¼ pound butter, softened
⅔ cup milk
1½ teaspoons vanilla extract
1 egg

1. Position rack in center of oven; preheat to 350°F. Melt butter in a saucepan. Sprinkle in brown sugar and stir to combine. Spoon mixture into cups of a 12-cup muffin pan, covering the bottom of each cup. Break off pieces of pineapple slices to form a smaller ring in the bottom of each cup (about ½ slice per cup). Place maraschino cherry half in center of each pineapple ring. Set aside.

2. In a large mixing bowl, stir together flour, sugar, baking powder, and salt. Using an electric mixer, beat in butter and milk on low speed until blended. Scrape down sides of bowl and beat on medium speed for

2 minutes. Add vanilla and egg, beating again for 2 minutes. Ladle batter into cups over pineapple, dividing batter evenly among cups.

3. Bake 30 minutes, or until a cake tester inserted in center of one cupcake comes out clean and cake springs back when pressed lightly in center. Remove pans from oven and place on wire racks for 4 to 5 minutes. Then, with a knife, go around edges of each cake to separate from side of pan. Invert onto a foil-covered cookie sheet, leaving pan over cakes for about 2 minutes. Remove pan and serve warm or cold with whipped cream.

Yield: 12 cupcakes

• STRAWBERRY SHORT CUPCAKES •

You'll love these tiny cakes with whipped cream and lots of juicy ripe strawberries.

2 pints strawberries
2 to 3 tablespoons sugar
2 cups sifted cake flour
2½ teaspoons baking powder
¼ teaspoon salt
⅓ cup shortening
1 cup sugar

1 teaspoon vanilla extract
1 egg
⅔ cup milk
1 cup heavy cream, whipped and
*   sweetened with 1 tablespoon*
*   sugar*

1. Slice strawberries into very thin pieces and mix with sugar for desired sweetness. Let stand at room temperature while you prepare cake.

2. Position rack in center of oven; preheat to 375°F. Grease a 12-cup muffin pan. In a medium mixing bowl, stir together flour, baking powder, and salt.

3. In a large mixing bowl and using an electric mixer, cream shortening until soft and smooth. Gradually add sugar, creaming until fluffy. Beat in vanilla and egg. Add flour alternately with milk, beating until smooth after each addition. Ladle batter into greased muffin pan, filling each cup about half full.

4. Bake 20 to 25 minutes, or until a cake tester inserted in center of one cupcake comes out clean and cake springs back when pressed lightly in

center. Remove pan from oven and place on wire rack for 5 minutes before turning cupcakes out onto racks. Reinvert immediately.

5. When cooled, use a serrated knife to slice tops off cupcakes. Mash half the sweetened strawberries and spoon equally on lower halves of cupcakes. Cover each one with a heaping teaspoon of whipped cream and cover with lid of cupcake. Cover with sliced strawberries and top with more whipped cream.

Yield: 18 cupcakes

· GERMAN CHOCOLATE CUPCAKES ·

This cupcake concept is adapted from Larry's family recipe for German chocolate cake.

½ cup water
1 (8-ounce) package sweet cooking
* chocolate*
½ pound butter, softened
2 cups granulated sugar
4 egg yolks

1 teaspoon vanilla extract
2½ cups sifted cake flour
1 teaspoon baking soda
1 cup buttermilk
4 egg whites

1. Position rack in center of oven; preheat to 350°F. Line two 12-cup muffin pans with paper cupcake liners.

2. In a saucepan, bring water to a boil and add chocolate. Stir until chocolate is melted. Set aside to cool.

3. In a large bowl and using an electric mixer, cream butter until soft, then gradually add sugar and beat until light and fluffy. Add egg yolks one at a time, beating thoroughly after each addition. Add chocolate and vanilla and mix on low speed until blended.

4. In a medium bowl, sift together flour and baking soda, then add alternately with buttermilk, beating well after each addition. Beat egg whites until stiff, then fold into batter. Ladle batter into pans, filling each cup three-quarters full.

5. Bake 30 to 35 minutes, or until a cake tester inserted in center of one cupcake comes out clean and cake springs back when pressed lightly in

center. Remove pans from oven and place on wire racks for 10 minutes before turning cupcakes out onto racks. Reinvert immediately.

FROSTING

½ cup heavy cream	4 tablespoons butter
¼ cup milk	1 teaspoon pure vanilla extract
¾ cup granulated sugar	1 cup shredded coconut
2 egg yolks	

In a saucepan, combine the heavy cream, milk, sugar, egg yolks, butter, and vanilla extract. Cook over medium heat about 10 minutes, stirring constantly until mixture thickens. Stir in coconut and remove from heat, continuing to stir until cool. Frost each cupcake.

Yield: 18 cupcakes

ANGEL FOOD CUPCAKES WITH WARM ♦ BITTERSWEET CHOCOLATE SAUCE

These light, fluffy, angel food cupcakes drizzled with hot bittersweet chocolate sauce and topped with whipped cream make an elegant dinner party dessert.

½ cup milk
2 tablespoons butter
4 egg whites
¼ teaspoon cream of tartar
1 cup sifted cake flour

1 teaspoon baking powder
¼ teaspoon salt
1 cup granulated sugar
1 teaspoon vanilla extract

1. Position rack in center of oven; preheat to 350°F. Line a 12-cup muffin pan with paper cupcake liners.

2. In a saucepan, slowly heat milk with butter to the scalding point, then remove pan from heat.

3. Beat eggs whites until frothy, add cream of tartar, and continue beating until whites form stiff peaks.

4. In a medium bowl, sift together flour, baking powder, and salt.

5. In a large mixing bowl and using an electric mixer, combine hot milk and sugar and beat on medium speed until frothy. On low speed, gradually add flour mixture and beat well. Fold in egg whites. Fold in vanilla. Ladle batter into pans, filling each cup three-quarters full.

6. Bake 25 to 30 minutes, or until a cake tester inserted in center of one cupcake comes out clean and cake springs back when pressed lightly in

center. Remove pan from oven and place on wire rack for 2 to 3 minutes before turning cupcakes out onto racks. Reinvert immediately to prevent cakes from sticking to racks. Serve cool with hot bittersweet chocolate sauce and whipped cream.

BITTERSWEET CHOCOLATE SAUCE

½ cup milk
½ cup heavy cream
2 ounces unsweetened chocolate
2 tablespoons granulated sugar

1 tablespoon unsalted butter
1 cup heavy cream, whipped and
* sweetened with 1 to 2*
* tablespoons granulated sugar*

Combine the milk, ½ cup cream, and chocolate in a saucepan over low heat, stirring occasionally, until chocolate is melted. Using a hand-held electric mixer, beat until soft and smooth. Blend in sugar, then add butter, stirring to melt. Cool until warm to the touch. Pour 1 tablespoon of warm sauce over each cupcake, then top with sweetened whipped cream.

Yield: 12 cupcakes

Chocolate Cupcakes

For those of you who love to eat chocolate and to bake with chocolate, here are more recipes to help satisfy your passions. (See Index for other chocolate cupcake recipes.)

◆ CHOCOLATE ANGEL FOOD CUPCAKES ◆

These feather-light cupcakes make ideal companions for fresh strawberries.

1 cup granulated sugar
¾ cup sifted cake flour
¼ cup unsweetened cocoa
¼ teaspoon salt

10 egg whites
1½ teaspoons vanilla extract
1½ teaspoons cream of tartar

1. Position rack in center of oven; preheat to 375°F. Line two 12-cup muffin pans with paper cupcake liners.

2. In a medium bowl, stir or whisk together ¾ cup of the sugar, the flour, cocoa, and salt. In a large mixing bowl and using an electric mixer, beat egg whites until frothy, add the vanilla and cream of tartar, and beat until soft peaks form. Gradually beat in remaining ¼ cup sugar, beating until stiff peaks form. Sift the flour mixture ¼ cup at a time over egg whites, gently folding in.

3. Pour or ladle (it is better to pour this mixture than to spoon so as not to disturb air bubbles) into pans, filling each cup two-thirds full.

4. Bake 30 to 35 minutes, or until a cake tester inserted in center of one cupcake comes out clean and cake springs back when pressed lightly in center. Remove pans from oven and place on wire racks. Let cupcakes cool completely in pans before turning them out onto counter. Dust with confectioners' sugar and serve with fresh strawberries.

Yield: 24 cupcakes

• CHOCOLATE NOUGAT CAKE •

Raisins are what make these cupcakes so moist and chewy. Serve with buttercream frosting or just by themselves.

CAKE

3 squares (3 ounces) unsweetened
   chocolate
¼ pound butter, softened
1 cup granulated sugar
2 eggs

1 teaspoon baking soda
1 cup buttermilk
1½ cups sifted cake flour
1 cup chopped raisins
1 teaspoon vanilla extract

1. Position rack in center of oven; preheat to 350°F. Line one 12-cup muffin pan with paper cupcake liners. Melt chocolate in top pan of a double boiler over hot water.

2. In a large bowl and using an electric mixer set on medium speed, cream butter until soft. Add sugar gradually, beating until light and fluffy. Add eggs one at a time, beating well after each addition.

3. Stir baking soda into buttermilk. Add with chocolate to creamed mixture, beating until blended. In a medium mixing bowl, stir together flour and raisins. Pour into batter, mixing on low speed until combined. Mix in vanilla. Ladle batter into pans, filling each cup two-thirds full.

4. Bake 30 minutes, or until a cake tester inserted in center of one cupcake comes out clean and cake springs back when pressed lightly in center. Remove pan from oven and place on wire racks for 5 minutes

before turning cupcakes out onto rack. Reinvert immediately to prevent cake from sticking to racks.

BUTTERCREAM FROSTING

¼ pound butter, softened	1 teaspoon vanilla extract
2 egg yolks	2 cups sifted confectioners' sugar

In a medium bowl and using an electric mixer, cream the butter until soft. Add egg yolks, one at a time, beating well after each addition. Blend in vanilla, then gradually add sugar, beating until desired spreading consistency is reached. You may not need to use all the sugar. Beat on high speed to remove curdles. Scrape down bowl. Frost cupcakes when they are thoroughly cool.

Yield: 12 cupcakes

• CARAMEL FUDGE CUPCAKES •

Here's a delightful combination—creamy fudge frosting on caramel-flavored cake. Yum!

1 cup granulated sugar	*¼ teaspoon salt*
½ cup boiling water	*½ cup shortening*
1½ cups sifted cake flour	*2 eggs, separated*
1½ teaspoons baking powder	*1 teaspoon vanilla extract*

1. Position rack in center of oven; preheat to 375°F. Line a 12-cup muffin pan with paper cupcake liners. Make caramel in a small saucepan by melting ½ cup of the sugar over medium heat, stirring constantly until golden brown. Remove from heat and gradually stir in boiling water. Return pan to heat and simmer until caramel is dissolved. Set aside.

2. In a medium bowl, stir or whisk together flour, baking powder, and salt. In a large bowl and using an electric mixer, cream shortening until smooth. Gradually add remaining 1½ cups sugar and beat until fluffy. Beat in egg yolks and vanilla.

3. Add flour mixture alternately with caramel syrup, beating smooth after each addition. In a separate bowl and using clean beaters, beat egg whites until stiff. Fold into batter. Ladle batter into pans, filling each cup two-thirds full.

4. Bake 20 minutes, or until a cake tester inserted in center of one cupcake comes out clean and cake springs back when pressed lightly in center. Remove pan from oven and place on wire rack for 5 minutes before

turning cupcakes out onto racks. Reinvert immediately. Cool thoroughly before frosting.

CHOCOLATE FUDGE FROSTING

2 squares (2 ounces) unsweetened
  chocolate
⅔ cup milk or light cream
2 cups granulated sugar

2 tablespoons light corn syrup
2 tablespoons butter
1 teaspoon vanilla extract

1. In a medium saucepan over low heat, combine chocolate and milk or light cream. Cooking slowly, stirring, until chocolate is melted and well blended with milk. Add sugar and corn syrup, stirring constantly until sugar is dissolved and mixture boils. Cover and boil for 3 minutes, then uncover and boil until a small amount forms a soft ball when dropped into a glass of cold water. Remove from heat, add butter and vanilla, then cool until lukewarm.

2. Using a hand-held electric mixer, beat mixture until creamy and thick enough to spread. If frosting is too thick, place over a pan of hot water to keep soft.

Yield: 12 cupcakes

. COCONUT CREAM–FILLED .
CHOCOLATE CUPCAKES

We love to watch our guests' faces when they bite into these moist chocolate cupcakes and discover the rich coconut filling inside. Once you try these, you'll bake them again and again.

COCONUT FILLING

4 ounces cream cheese	1 egg
1/3 cup granulated sugar	1/2 cup coconut

CAKE

1/2 pound plus 4 tablespoons butter, softened	2 cups sifted cake flour
1 cup granulated sugar	2 teaspoons baking soda
1 egg	1/4 teaspoon salt
3/4 cup unsweetened cocoa	1 1/2 cups milk

1. Position rack in center of oven; preheat to 350°F. Line two 12-cup muffin pans with paper cupcake liners.

2. In small bowl and using an electric mixer, beat cream cheese and sugar until fluffy. Beat in egg until well blended. Stir in coconut and set aside.

3. In a large bowl and using an electric mixer, cream butter with sugar, beating until light and fluffy. Beat in egg. In a medium bowl, stir or

whisk together cocoa, flour, baking soda, and salt. Add dry ingredients alternately with milk to creamed mixture, beating until smooth and well blended. Pour half the batter into pans, filling each cup half full. Spoon one heaping ½ teaspoon coconut filling into center of each cup of batter. Cover with remaining cake batter until two-thirds full.

4. Bake 20 minutes, or until a cake tester inserted in center of one cupcake comes out clean and cake springs back when pressed lightly in center. Remove pans from oven and place on wire racks for 5 minutes before turning cupcakes out onto racks. Reinvert immediately to prevent cakes from sticking to racks. Frost with Basic Butter Frosting.

BASIC BUTTER FROSTING
4 tablespoons butter, softened
2 cups sifted confectioners' sugar

1 teaspoon vanilla extract
3 to 4 tablespoons cream

In a small bowl and using an electric mixer, cream butter until soft. Gradually beat in 1 cup of the sugar. Add vanilla. Alternately add remaining sugar and cream, beating smooth after each addition, adding enough cream for desired spreading consistency.

Yield: 24 cupcakes

• CHOCOLATE SPICE CUPCAKES •

The nutmeg is in the cake, the cloves and cinnamon are in the chocolate frosting—a cozy combination.

¼ pound butter, softened
1½ cups granulated sugar
3 eggs, beaten
2 cups sifted cake flour
¼ teaspoon salt

1 teaspoon baking powder
¼ teaspoon baking soda
2 teaspoons nutmeg
1 cup buttermilk

1. Position rack in center of oven; preheat to 350°F. Line two 12-cup muffin pans with paper cupcake liners.

2. In a large mixing bowl and using an electric mixer, cream butter until soft. Gradually add sugar, beating until light and fluffy. Beat in well-beaten eggs.

3. In a medium bowl, stir or whisk together flour, salt, baking powder, baking soda, and nutmeg. Add alternately with buttermilk to creamed mixture, beating until smooth and well blended. Ladle into pans, filling each cup two-thirds full.

4. Bake 25 minutes, or until a cake tester inserted in center of one cupcake comes out clean and cake springs back when pressed lightly in center. Remove pans from oven and place on wire racks for 10 minutes before turning cupcakes out onto racks. Reinvert immediately. Frost with Chocolate Cinnamon Frosting when cupcakes are completely cool.

CHOCOLATE CINNAMON FROSTING

3 squares (3 ounces) unsweetened
   chocolate
4 tablespoons butter, softened
1½ cups sifted confectioners' sugar

½ teaspoon cinnamon
1/16 teaspoon ground cloves
¼ teaspoon vanilla extract
2 egg whites

1. Melt chocolate in top pan of a double boiler over hot water.

2. In a medium bowl and using an electric mixer, cream butter until soft. With mixer on medium speed, add ½ cup of the sugar, beating constantly. Add melted chocolate, cinnamon, clove, and vanilla, beating until smooth.

3. In a separate bowl and using clean beaters, beat egg whites until stiff. Gradually beat in remaining 1 cup of sugar. Gradually beat egg whites into creamed mixture, beating until frosting is stiff and holds shape.

Yield: 18 cupcakes

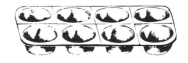

• CHOCOLATE ORANGE CUPCAKES •

If you love the delightful combination of orange and chocolate, you'll want to try these cupcakes.

2¼ cups sifted cake flour
1 cup granulated sugar
2 teaspoons baking powder
¼ teaspoon baking soda
½ teaspoon salt
¼ pound butter, softened

2 teaspoons grated orange rind
¼ cup freshly squeezed orange juice
  (with pulp)
¾ cup water
2 eggs

1. Position rack in center of oven; preheat to 350°F. Line two 12-cup muffin pans with paper cupcake liners.

2. In a large mixing bowl, stir or whisk together flour, sugar, baking powder, baking soda, and salt. Using an electric mixer, beat in butter and orange rind. Mix together orange juice and water. Pour ⅔ cup juice mixture into batter. Beat for 2 minutes on high speed. Beat in remaining orange juice mixture and eggs. Beat 2 more minutes. Ladle into pans, filling each cup two-thirds full.

3. Bake 20 to 25 minutes, or until a cake tester inserted in center of one cupcake comes out clean and cake springs back when pressed lightly in center. Remove pans from oven and place on wire racks for 5 minutes before turning cupcakes out onto racks. Reinvert immediately. Frost with Chocolate Fudge Frosting.

CHOCOLATE FUDGE FROSTING

4 squares (4 ounces) unsweetened chocolate	3¼ cups sifted confectioners' sugar
¼ pound butter, softened	1 teaspoon vanilla extract
	¼ cup milk

1. Using a double boiler, melt chocolate in top pan over hot water, stirring frequently until smooth. Remove chocolate pan from hot water and let cool for 5 minutes.

2. In a large bowl and using an electric mixer, beat the butter until soft. On medium speed, gradually beat in half the sugar until frosting is stiff. Add the chocolate and vanilla. Alternately add milk and remaining sugar until desired spreading consistency is reached.

Yield: 24 cupcakes

Fruit and Nut Cupcakes

· PINEAPPLE ORANGE CUPCAKES ·

These cupcakes are mouthwateringly delicious.

4 tablespoons butter, melted
2 cups granulated sugar
4 eggs, separated
Grated rind of 1 orange

1 teaspoon vanilla extract
1 cup milk
3 cups sifted cake flour
2½ teaspoons baking powder

1. Position rack in center of oven; preheat to 375°F. Line two 12-cup muffin pans with paper cupcake liners.

2. In a large mixing bowl and using an electric mixer, cream butter until soft. Gradually add sugar, beating until light and fluffy. Mix in egg yolks, one at a time, beating well after each addition. Blend in orange rind and vanilla.

3. In a medium bowl, beat egg whites until stiff. Fold into batter until combined. Ladle batter into pans, filling each cup two-thirds full.

4. Bake 20 minutes, or until a cake tester inserted in center of one cupcake comes out clean and cake springs back when pressed lightly in center. Remove pans from oven and place on wire racks for 5 minutes before turning cupcakes out onto racks. Reinvert immediately. When cupcakes are completely cool, frost with Pineapple Frosting.

PINEAPPLE FROSTING
½ cup canned crushed pineapple,
    well drained

5⅓ tablespoons butter, softened
2½ to 3 cups confectioners' sugar

Drain pineapple. In a medium mixing bowl and using an electric mixer, cream butter until soft. Gradually add sugar for desired spreading consistency. Stir in pineapple until well blended.

Yield: 18 cupcakes

• ORANGE-GLAZED PECAN CUPCAKES •

CAKE

2½ cups sifted all-purpose flour
2 teaspoons baking powder
½ teaspoon baking soda
½ teaspoon salt
2 teaspoons vanilla extract
1 tablespoon grated orange rind
1 cup sour cream

½ pound butter, softened
½ cup granulated sugar
1 cup firmly packed light brown sugar
4 eggs
1½ cups finely chopped pecans

1. Position rack in center of oven; preheat to 350°F. Line two 12-cup muffin pans with paper cupcake liners.

2. In a medium mixing bowl, stir or whisk together flour, baking powder, baking soda, and salt. In a small bowl, stir together vanilla, orange rind, and sour cream. Set aside.

3. In a large mixing bowl and using an electric mixer, cream butter until smooth. Gradually add the granulated sugar, then the brown sugar, and continue beating on high speed until the mixture is light and fluffy. On medium speed, add the eggs, one at a time, beating well after each addition. Now on low speed, alternately beat in the sifted dry ingredients and the sour cream mixture, beating only until ingredients are combined. Stir in nuts. Pour batter into pans, filling each cup two-thirds full.

4. Bake 25 minutes, or until a cake tester inserted in center of one cupcake comes out clean and cake springs back when pressed lightly in

center. Remove pans from oven and place on wire racks for 10 minutes before turning cupcakes out onto racks. Reinvert immediately to prevent cakes from sticking to racks. Glaze cupcakes while still warm.

ORANGE GLAZE

1⅓ cups sifted confectioners' sugar	2 teaspoons orange rind
4 tablespoons orange juice	

In a small bowl, combine sugar, orange juice, and orange rind, stirring briskly until smooth and well blended. Brush generously over warm cupcakes. Serve when cool.

Yield: 24 cupcakes

• MAPLE WALNUT CUPCAKES •

For the best flavor, use pure maple syrup. It may cost more, but it's worth it.

¼ pound butter, softened
½ cup maple syrup
2 eggs
2 cups sifted cake flour

½ cup water
4 teaspoons baking powder
½ teaspoon salt

1. Position rack in center of oven; preheat to 375°F. Line two 12-cup muffin pans with paper cupcake liners.

2. In a large bowl and using an electric mixer, cream butter until soft. Add maple syrup gradually, beating on low speed until combined. Add one egg at a time, beating well after each addition.

3. Add 1 cup of the flour alternately with ¼ cup of the water. Beat until smooth. Add remaining flour, baking powder, and salt. Beat in remaining water until well combined. Ladle into pans, filling each cup half full.

4. Bake 15 to 20 minutes, or until a cake tester inserted in center of one cupcake comes out clean and cake springs back when pressed lightly in center. Remove pans from oven and place on wire racks for 5 minutes before turning cupcakes out onto racks. Reinvert immediately to prevent cakes from sticking to racks. Frost when thoroughly cool.

MAPLE WALNUT FROSTING
2½ cups sifted confectioners' sugar   *3 to 4 tablespoons maple syrup*

2 tablespoons butter, softened   *¾ cup finely chopped walnuts*
¼ teaspoon vanilla extract

In a medium bowl and using an electric mixer, combine sugar and butter, beating until smooth. Blend in vanilla. On medium speed, blend in maple syrup one tablespoon at a time to create desired spreading consistency. Frost cupcakes, then sprinkle generously with chopped walnuts.

Yield: 18 cupcakes

• BANANA NUT CUPCAKES •

Our dear friend Carol Farnsworth shared this recipe with us. It's a favorite in her family, and now it is in ours. We have her grandmother, Theda Mercer, to thank for it.

1 cup mashed, very ripe bananas	*2 cups sifted all-purpose flour*
1 tablespoon lemon juice	*½ teaspoon salt*
¼ pound butter, softened	*1 teaspoon baking soda*
1 cup granulated sugar	*1 teaspoon water*
2 eggs	*½ cup chopped walnuts*

1. Position rack in center of oven; preheat to 350°F. Line two 12-cup muffin pans with paper cupcake liners. In a small bowl, mash bananas with lemon juice.

2. In a large mixing bowl and using an electric mixer, cream together butter and sugar until light and fluffy. Beat in eggs until combined. In a medium bowl, stir or whisk together flour and salt. Gradually add dry ingredients to creamed mixture until ingredients are moistened. Dissolve baking soda in the water and blend into mixture until smooth. Stir in walnuts. Ladle batter into pans, filling each cup two-thirds full.

3. Bake 30 minutes, or until a cake tester inserted in center of one cupcake comes out clean and cake springs back when pressed lightly in center. Remove pans from oven and place on wire racks for 5 minutes before turning cupcakes out onto racks. Reinvert immediately. Serve plain or with Cream Cheese Frosting.

EASY CREAM CHEESE FROSTING

2 (3-ounce) packages cream cheese, softened
2 tablespoons butter, softened
2 teaspoons vanilla extract

3½ to 4 cups sifted confectioners' sugar
1 to 2 tablespoons milk, as needed

In a small mixing bowl and using an electric mixer, cream together cream cheese, butter, and vanilla. Gradually add sugar, beating until fluffy. If frosting is too thick, add milk as needed to create desired spreading consistency. Spread on thoroughly cool cupcakes.

Yield: 18 cupcakes

· LEMON MERINGUE CUPCAKES ·

Simply stated, these cupcakes are *so* good! If you enjoy lemon meringue pie, you'll love this deliciously lemony cupcake variation.

LEMON FILLING
4 egg yolks
½ tablespoon cornstarch
⅓ cup plus 1 tablespoon sugar

⅓ cup lemon juice
¾ cup whipping cream

1. Position rack in center of oven; preheat to 225°F.
2. In a medium bowl, beat egg yolks lightly. In a small bowl, stir together the cornstarch and sugar, then gradually blend them into the egg yolks. Gradually whisk in lemon juice. In a saucepan over medium heat, bring cream to a boil, stirring occasionally. When cream is boiling, pour in lemon mixture, stirring until blended. Remove from heat. Pour into a small glass baking dish and bake for 45 minutes. Remove dish from oven and place on a wire rack to cool. Filling will thicken as it cools. Increase oven temperature to 350° F for baking the cake.

CAKE
2 cups sifted cake flour
2 teaspoons baking powder
¼ teaspoon salt
¼ pound butter, softened

1⅓ cups granulated sugar
1½ teaspoons vanilla extract
⅔ cup milk
4 eggs whites

1. Line two 12-cup muffin pans with paper cupcake liners. In a medium bowl, mix or whisk together flour, baking powder, and salt.

2. In a large bowl and using an electric mixer, cream butter until smooth and light. Gradually add 1 cup of the sugar, creaming until mixture is fluffy.

3. Add dry ingredients alternately with milk and vanilla, beating until smooth after each addition.

4. Beat egg whites until stiff, gradually beating in remaining ⅓ cup sugar. Fold mixture thoroughly into cake batter.

5. Pour batter into cupcake pan, filling each cup two-thirds full. Bake 25 minutes, or until a cake tester inserted in center of one cupcake comes out clean and cake springs back when pressed lightly in center. Remove pans from oven and place on wire racks for 5 minutes before turning cupcakes out onto racks. Reinvert immediately.

EASY MERINGUE TOPPING
4 egg whites   *6 tablespoons granulated sugar*
¼ teaspoon cream of tartar

1. In a medium mixing bowl and using an electric mixer, beat the egg whites until light and frothy. Add cream of tartar and continue beating until the whites are stiff enough to hold peaks. Gradually beat in sugar and beat until stiff.

2. Using a serrated knife, carefully slice tops off cooled cupcakes. Scoop a spoonful of cake from centers and spoon a tablespoon of lemon filling in each cake. Replace tops, spread a very thin layer of filling on top of

cupcakes, then cover with meringue topping, using back of a spoon to swirl meringue into a single peak. Turn on broiler. Place cupcakes on a cookie sheet and place under broiler for only 2 to 3 seconds, or just enough to brown meringue, being careful not to burn.

Yield: 18 cupcakes

· DATE NUT CUPCAKES ·

Enjoy these cupcakes served warm and spread with cream cheese.

1 cup boiling water
1 cup finely chopped dates
1/4 pound butter, softened
1 cup firmly packed light brown
  sugar
2 eggs

2 cups flour
1 teaspoon baking powder
1 teaspoon baking soda
1/2 teaspoon salt
1 teaspoon vanilla extract
1/2 cup chopped walnuts

1. Position rack in center of oven; preheat to 325°F. Line a 12-cup muffin pan with paper cupcake liners. Pour boiling water over dates. Let stand until cool.

2. In a large mixing bowl and using an electric mixer, cream butter until soft. Gradually add sugar, beating until light and fluffy. Add eggs one at a time, beating well after each addition.

3. In a medium bowl, stir together flour, baking powder, baking soda, and salt. Add alternately with water and dates to butter-sugar mixture, mixing until ingredients are moistened. Blend in vanilla. Fold in nuts. Ladle batter into pans, filling cups three-quarters full.

4. Bake 25 to 30 minutes, or until cake springs back when pressed lightly in center. Remove pan from oven and place on a wire rack for 10 minutes before turning cupcakes out onto rack. Reinvert immediately to prevent cakes from sticking to racks. Serve plain or with cream cheese.

Yield: 10 to 12 cupcakes

Coffee Cake
Cupcakes

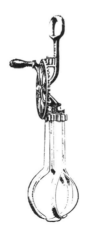

The clear and simple recipes in this chapter provide a welcome excuse to pause from our daily routine to celebrate the lost art of coffee breaks. All of these coffee cake cupcakes are quick and easy to make, leaving you more time to socialize with friends and family.

Coffee cake cupcakes are convenient to pack for work or school and make delightful fare at Sunday brunches or informal get-togethers. So, come on, fill your kitchen with the warm smell of cinnamon, put on a pot of coffee, and invite a friend over for one of these homey little cakes.

• WALNUT-FILLED COFFEE CUPCAKES •

FILLING

½ cup firmly packed light brown
 sugar
2 teaspoons cinnamon

1 cup finely chopped walnuts
2 tablespoons all-purpose flour
2 tablespoons butter, melted

CAKE

2 tablespoons butter, softened
½ cup granulated sugar
1 egg, separated
¾ cup sifted all-purpose flour

2 teaspoons baking powder
¼ cup milk
½ teaspoon vanilla extract

1. Position rack in center of oven; preheat to 350°F. Line a 12-cup muffin pan with paper cupcake liners.

2. In a medium bowl, combine brown sugar, cinnamon, walnuts, and flour. Stir in melted butter until all ingredients are well combined. Set aside.

3. In a large mixing bowl and using an electric mixer, cream butter and sugar until light and fluffy. Beat egg yolk and add to mixture.

4. In a medium mixing bowl, stir or whisk together flour and baking powder. Add alternately with milk to butter mixture, beating until smooth. Blend in vanilla.

5. In a small bowl, beat egg white until stiff, then fold into batter. Ladle half the batter into pans. Spread half the filling over top. Add remaining batter and top with rest of filling.

6. Bake 35 to 40 minutes, or until a cake tester inserted in center of one cupcake comes out clean. Remove pan from oven and place on wire rack for 10 minutes, then use a knife as a wedge to lift cakes out of pans with hands. Remove to rack and serve warm or cool.

Yield: 12 cupcakes

• ALMOND-COCONUT COFFEE CUPCAKES •

TOPPING
½ cup chopped almonds
½ cup flaked coconut

*½ cup firmly packed light brown
sugar*

CAKE
1¼ cups granulated sugar
*½ pound plus 4 tablespoons butter,
softened*
3 eggs
⅓ cup milk
⅓ cup almond paste

¼ teaspoon salt
1 teaspoon almond extract
2½ cups sifted cake flour
2 teaspoon baking powder
2 egg whites

1. Position rack in center of oven; preheat to 325°F. Line two 12-cup muffin pans with paper cupcake liners.

2. In a small bowl, combine nuts, coconut, and brown sugar. Stir until well blended. Set aside.

3. In a large bowl and using an electric mixer, cream 1 cup of the sugar and butter together until light and fluffy. Beat in the 3 eggs, one at a time, until well blended. Add milk, almond paste, salt, and almond extract. Beat until blended.

4. In a medium bowl, stir or whisk together flour and baking powder. Stir into batter until ingredients are moist.

5. Beat egg whites until frothy. Gradually add remaining ¼ cup sugar,

beating egg whites until stiff. Fold into batter. Ladle batter into pans, filling each cup two-thirds full. Sprinkle with topping.

6. Bake 35 to 40 minutes, or until a cake tester inserted in center of one cupcake comes out clean. Remove pans from oven and place on wire racks for 10 minutes, then, using knife as a wedge, lift cupcakes out with hands. Continue cooling on racks.

Yield: 18 cupcakes

• APPLE NUT COFFEE CUPCAKES •

This recipe comes from Catherine's grandmother, Mary Odell. She used to make it with fresh-picked apples from her orchard.

CAKE

1/4 pound butter, softened
1 cup granulated sugar
2 eggs
1 teaspoon vanilla extract
2 cups sifted all-purpose flour

1 teaspoon baking powder
1 teaspoon baking soda
1/4 teaspoon salt
1 cup sour cream
2 cups finely chopped apples

TOPPING

1/2 cup chopped nuts
1/2 cup firmly packed light brown
   sugar

1 teaspoon cinnamon
2 tablespoons butter, melted

1. Position rack in center of oven; preheat to 350°F. Line two 12-cup muffin pans with paper cupcake liners.

2. In a large mixing bowl and using an electric mixer, cream together butter and sugar, beating until light and fluffy. Add eggs, one at a time, beating until well blended. Beat in vanilla.

3. In a medium bowl, stir or whisk together flour, baking powder, baking soda, and salt. Add dry ingredients alternately with sour cream to creamed mixture. Fold in apples. Spoon batter into pans, filling each cup two-thirds full.

4. Prepare topping in a small bowl by combining nuts, brown sugar, cinnamon, and melted butter. Stir until well blended. Sprinkle over batter, dividing equally among all cups.

5. Bake 30 to 35 minutes, or until a cake tester inserted in center of one cupcake comes out clean. Remove pans from oven and place on wire racks for 10 minutes, then, using a knife as a wedge, lift cupcakes out of pans onto wire racks. Let cool.

Yield: 18 cupcakes

· DELICIOUS PRUNE CUPCAKES ·

Catherine's father wouldn't let us write this book without including a prune coffee cake recipe. This one is an adaptation of his mother's Slovak prune cake recipe.

1 cup finely chopped cooked prunes	*1 teaspoon baking soda*
¼ pound butter, softened	*1 teaspoon cinnamon*
1 cup granulated sugar	*½ teaspoon nutmeg*
2 eggs, well beaten	*½ cup sour cream*
1½ cups sifted cake flour	*1 teaspoon vanilla extract*

1. Position rack in center of oven; preheat to 350°F. Line a 12-cup muffin pan with paper cupcake liners.

2. In a saucepan, cover prunes with water and simmer for 15 to 20 minutes, until soft. Drain well and chop into small pieces.

3. In a large mixing bowl and using an electric mixer, cream butter until soft. Gradually add sugar, beating until light and fluffy. Beat in eggs until blended.

4. In a medium bowl, stir or whisk together flour, baking soda, cinnamon, and nutmeg. Add alternately with sour cream to creamed mixture until ingredients are moistened. Beat in vanilla. Stir in prunes. Batter will be heavy. Spoon into pans, filling each cup three-quarters full. Spread batter smooth with back of spoon.

5. Bake 25 to 30 minutes, or until a cake tester inserted in center of one

cupcake comes out clean. Remove pan from oven and place on wire rack for 10 minutes before turning cupcakes out onto racks. Reinvert immediately.

Yield: 12 cupcakes

· POPPY SEED CUPCAKES ·

These cupcakes are nice and light with a refreshing lemon glaze. As a time-saver, soak the poppy seeds overnight, so they'll be ready for the batter the next morning.

1 cup poppy seeds
1 cup milk
2 cups sifted all-purpose flour
2½ teaspoons baking powder
¼ teaspoon salt

¼ pound plus 4 tablespoons butter, softened
1¼ cups granulated sugar
4 eggs, separated
1 teaspoon vanilla extract

1. Prepare poppy seeds by combining seeds and milk in a small saucepan and bringing mixture to a simmer. Remove from heat and let stand for 25 to 30 minutes, to let seeds absorb milk. (Another method is to let poppy seeds stand in milk overnight, covered and refrigerated.)

2. Position rack in center of oven; preheat to 350°F. Line two 12-cup muffin pans with paper cupcake liners.

3. In a medium bowl, stir or whisk together flour, baking powder, and salt. Stir in poppy seed mixture.

4. In a large bowl and using an electric mixer, cream butter until soft. Gradually add sugar, beating until light and fluffy. Beat egg yolks and add with vanilla, beating until well combined. With mixer on low speed, gradually add flour mixture, turning to medium speed to beat until smooth.

5. In a separate bowl, beat egg whites until stiff. Gently fold into batter. Ladle batter into pans, filling each cup two-thirds full.

6. Bake 35 to 40 minutes, or until a cake tester inserted in center of one cupcake comes out clean and cake springs back when pressed lightly in center. Remove pans from oven and place on wire racks for 5 minutes before turning cupcakes out onto racks. Reinvert immediately to prevent cakes from sticking to racks. Prepare glaze and apply while cupcakes are still warm.

LEMON GLAZE
1 cup sifted confectioners' sugar
2 teaspoons fresh lemon juice

1 teaspoon freshly grated lemon rind

Combine sugar, lemon juice, and lemon rind in a small bowl, stirring until very smooth. Brush on warm cupcakes.

Yield: 24 cupcakes

• LEMON-BLUEBERRY CRUMB CUPCAKES •

Serve these coffee cupcakes warm to enjoy the luscious taste of fresh blueberries.

CRUMB TOPPING
3 tablespoons butter
½ cup all-purpose flour
⅓ cup sugar

1½ cups fresh blueberries, washed
and drained

CAKE
1½ cups sifted all-purpose flour
1 teaspoon baking powder
¼ teaspoon salt
4 tablespoons butter, softened
1 teaspoon vanilla extract

¾ cup sugar
1 egg
⅔ cup milk
Rind of 1 lemon, finely grated

1. Position rack in center of oven; preheat to 350°F. Line a 6-cup muffin pan with paper cupcake liners.

2. In a small bowl, combine butter, flour, and sugar. Use a fork to mash butter into flour and sugar, then stir until crumbs form. Gently stir in blueberries. Set aside.

3. In a medium bowl, sift together flour, baking powder, and salt. Set aside.

4. In a small bowl and using an electric mixer, beat the butter until

soft, then beat in vanilla. Gradually beat in sugar, then egg. On low speed, alternately add dry ingredients and milk, beating until ingredients are moistened. Stir in grated lemon rind. Spoon into pans, filling each cup half full. Smooth batter with spoon, then sprinkle evenly with blueberry crumb topping.

5. Bake 40 minutes, or until lightly browned. Remove pan from oven and place on wire rack for 10 minutes, then, using a knife as a wedge, lift cupcakes from pans onto racks. Serve warm.

Yield: 6 cupcakes

Healthy Cupcakes

When we first started telling people about our cupcake book, quite often people would ask if we were going to include recipes for healthy cupcakes, meaning low-cholesterol, fat-free, etc. It seemed to us that the term "healthy cupcake" was an oxymoron. Aren't cupcakes *supposed* to be sinfully delicious?

Fortunately, through our research, we have discovered this not to be the case. The best thing cupcakes have going for them is their serving size. Cupcake portions are inherently smaller than the average piece of cake. According to the American Heart Association, the typical white cupcake (2½ inches in diameter) has less than half the fat, calories, cholesterol, and sodium than the average piece of white layer cake (one sixteenth of a 9-inch diameter cake). There's something about having a little cake all to yourself that is psychologically very satisfying.

The recipes in this chapter have three things in common. They are cholesterol-free, contain no more than 1 gram of saturated fat per serving, and they all taste great. Enjoy!

• APPLESAUCE CUPCAKES •

Enjoy this cake with coffee or tea. Its warm flavors will remind you of an autumn harvest.

2 egg whites
½ cup light vegetable oil
1 cup granulated sugar
1½ cups sifted cake flour
¼ teaspoon salt
1 teaspoon baking soda

1 teaspoon cinnamon
½ teaspoon ground cloves
½ cup chopped walnuts
1 cup raisins
1 cup sweetened applesauce, heated

1. Position rack in center of oven; preheat to 350°F. Line two 12-cup muffin pans with paper cupcake liners.

2. In a large mixing bowl and using an electric mixer, beat egg whites until foamy. Blend in oil. In a medium bowl, stir or whisk together sugar, 1¼ cups of the cake flour, salt, baking soda, cinnamon, and cloves.

3. Sift remaining ¼ cup flour over walnuts and raisins. Stir into batter. In a saucepan, heat applesauce until warm, then blend into batter. Pour into pans, filling each cup two-thirds full.

4. Bake 30 to 35 minutes, or until a cake tester inserted in center of one cupcake comes out clean and cake springs back when pressed lightly in center. Remove pans from oven and place on wire racks for 10 minutes before turning cupcakes out onto racks. Reinvert immediately. Serve warm.

Yield: 18 cupcakes

· CHOCOLATE MOCHA CUPCAKES ·

Light chocolate cake with delicious mocha frosting make this cupcake melt-in-your-mouth good.

¼ cup light vegetable oil, such as
   corn or safflower oil
2½ cups firmly packed light brown
   sugar
5 egg whites
½ cup buttermilk
2 teaspoons vanilla extract
2¼ cups sifted cake flour

¼ teaspoon salt
⅓ cup unsweetened cocoa
1 teaspoon baking soda
1 cup boiling water

1. Position rack in center of oven; preheat to 375°F. Line two 12-cup muffin pans with paper cupcake liners.

2. In a large bowl and using an electric mixer, cream together oil and brown sugar. On low speed, blend in egg whites, buttermilk, and vanilla. In a medium bowl, stir or whisk together flour, salt, and cocoa. Add dry ingredients to batter in four batches, blending well after each addition. Dissolve baking soda in the boiling water and stir into batter. Beat well. Pour batter into pans, filling each cup two-thirds full.

3. Bake 20 minutes, or until a cake tester inserted in center of one cupcake comes out clean and cake springs back when pressed lightly in center. Remove pans from oven and place on wire racks for 10 minutes before turning cupcakes out onto racks. Reinvert immediately to prevent

cakes from sticking to racks. When cupcakes are completely cool, frost with Mocha Frosting.

MOCHA FROSTING

⅔ cup firmly packed light brown sugar
¼ cup brewed coffee (or made from instant)

2 egg whites
¼ teaspoon cream of tartar
1 teaspoon vanilla extract

1. In a small saucepan, combine brown sugar and coffee. Without stirring, bring to a boil, then cover and continue boiling for 3 minutes. Uncover and boil until syrup makes a thin thread when dropped from the side of a metal spoon.

2. In a medium bowl and using an electric mixer, beat egg whites until frothy. Add cream of tartar. Continue beating until egg whites are stiff. Pour hot syrup into beaten egg whites, beating constantly. Add vanilla. Beat until the frosting peaks and is desired spreading consistency.

Yield: 18 cupcakes

• ORANGE SPICE CUPCAKES •

The refreshing orange frosting perfectly complements the cinnamon and clove in this spicy cupcake.

CAKE

½ cup light oil, such as safflower
  or corn oil
¾ cup granulated sugar
¾ cup firmly packed light brown
  sugar
2 cups sifted cake flour
2 teaspoons baking powder

¼ teaspoon salt
½ teaspoon ground cloves
1 teaspoon cinnamon
¾ cup milk
1 teaspoon vanilla extract
4 egg whites

1. Position rack in center of oven; preheat to 350°F. Line two 12-cup muffin pans with paper cupcake liners.

2. In a large bowl and using an electric mixer, cream together oil, granulated sugar, and brown sugar. In a medium bowl, stir or whisk together flour, baking powder, salt, cloves, and cinnamon. Combine milk and vanilla.

3. Add dry ingredients and milk alternately to creamed mixture, beating slightly after each addition. In a small bowl and using clean beaters, beat egg whites until stiff. Fold into batter. Pour batter into pans, filling each cup two-thirds full.

4. Bake 15 to 20 minutes, or until a cake tester inserted in center of one

cupcake comes out clean and cake springs back when pressed lightly in center. Remove pans from oven and place on wire racks for 10 minutes before turning cupcakes out onto racks. Reinvert immediately. When cupcakes are completely cool, frost with Orange Frosting.

ORANGE FROSTING

2 cups sifted confectioners' sugar	3 tablespoons orange juice
1 tablespoon skim milk	1 tablespoon lemon juice
1 tablespoon light oil	¼ teaspoon grated orange rind

In the top of a double boiler over hot water, combine all ingredients, stirring until blended. Let ingredients sit until they are warm; do not boil. Using an electric mixer, beat frosting until smooth. If frosting is too thick, thin with skim milk to desired spreading consistency.

Yield: 24 cupcakes

• LEMON LIFTS •

Citrus lovers rejoice! Enjoy the fresh lemon flavor of this light cake with an orange-lemon glaze.

½ cup light vegetable oil
1½ cups granulated sugar
2 cups sifted cake flour
2 teaspoons baking powder
½ teaspoon salt

¼ cup water
½ cup freshly squeezed lemon juice
Grated rind of 1 lemon
4 egg whites

1. Position rack in center of oven; preheat to 350°F. Line two 12-cup muffin pans with paper cupcake liners.

2. In a large bowl and using an electric mixer, cream together oil and sugar until light and fluffy. In a medium bowl, stir or whisk together flour, baking powder, and salt. Combine water and lemon juice.

3. Alternately add the dry ingredients and lemon juice mixture to the creamed mixture, beating well after each addition. Stir in lemon rind. In a separate bowl and using clean beaters, beat egg whites until stiff. Fold into batter. Pour into pans, filling each cup two-thirds full.

4. Bake 20 minutes, or until a cake tester inserted in center of one cupcake comes out clean and cake springs back when pressed lightly in center. Remove pans from oven and place on wire racks for 5 minutes before turning cupcakes out onto racks. When cupcakes are cool, reinvert them and frost with Citrus Glaze.

CITRUS GLAZE

1 cup sifted confectioners' sugar
½ teaspoon finely grated orange rind
½ teaspoon finely grated lemon rind

1 tablespoon freshly squeezed lemon juice
2 to 3 tablespoons freshly squeezed orange juice

Combine all ingredients, stirring until smooth. Add more orange juice if too thick. Brush on cooled cupcakes.

Yield: 18 cupcakes

· STRAWBERRY PATCH ANGEL FOOD CUPCAKES ·

If you use really ripe strawberries in this recipe you can decrease the amount of sugar in the meringue.

¾ cup sifted cake flour	*¾ teaspoon cream of tartar*
1 cup granulated sugar	*¼ teaspoon salt*
7 medium egg whites	*¾ teaspoon vanilla extract*

1. Position rack in center of oven; preheat to 375°F. Line a 12-cup muffin pan with paper cupcake liners.

2. In a medium bowl, stir or whisk together flour and 2 tablespoons of the sugar.

3. Using an electric mixer, beat egg whites until frothy. Beat in cream of tartar, salt, and vanilla. Beat until peaks form. Sprinkle remaining sugar over surface of egg whites, 2 tablespoons at a time, and fold in with a rubber spatula. Sift ¼ cup of flour mixture over surface and fold in. Repeat until all flour is added. Gently spoon or pour batter into pans, filling each cup two-thirds full.

4. Bake 15 minutes, or until a cake tester inserted in center of one cupcake comes out clean and cake springs back when pressed lightly in center. Remove pan from oven and place on a wire rack until cupcakes are completely cooled. Remove cupcakes from pan and serve with Strawberry Patch Meringue.

STRAWBERRY PATCH MERINGUE

1 cup fresh strawberries, hulled
* and mashed*
⅔ cup granulated sugar

⅛ teaspoon cream of tartar
2 egg whites

In a medium mixing bowl and using an electric mixer, combine mashed strawberries, sugar, cream of tartar, and egg whites. Beat at high speed for 8 to 10 minutes, until mixture forms peaks. If it is tart, add a little more sugar.

Yield: 12 cupcakes.

Index

Italics indicate names of recipes

Almond-Coconut Coffee Cupcakes, 109–10
Angel food cupcakes, 74–75, 79, 128–29
*Angel Food Cupcakes with Warm
    Bittersweet Chocolate Sauce*, 74–75
Apple Nut Coffee Cupcakes, 111–12
Applesauce Cupcakes, 121
Aprons, 27–28

Bake cups
    filling, 19, 23
    fluted paper, 4, 9
    origin of, 4–5
    reasons for using, 4
    size and fit of, 9
Baking powder, testing freshness of, 12,
    15
Baking soda, 15
Baking time, 19
Baking with children, 26–29
Banana Nut Cupcakes, 98–99
Baseball Butterscotch Cupcakes, 46–47
Basic Butter Frosting, 85
Beat (term), 20
Bittersweet Chocolate Sauce, 75
Black Forest Cupcakes, 66–67
Blend (term), 20
Bowls, 10
Butter, 14

Buttercream Frosting, 81
Butterscotch cupcakes, 46
Butterscotch Frosting, 47

Cake flour, converting all-purpose flour
    to, 12–13
Cake recipes, 2
Cake tester, 12
Caramel Fudge Cupcakes, 82–83
Carrot cupcakes, 56–57
Chemistry of cupcakes, 12–17
Children
    baking cupcakes with, 26–29
    favorite recipes of, 30–60
Chocolate
    cupcakes with, 30, 38, 54, 58, 64, 66,
        72, 77–89, 122
    frostings with, 43, 53, 59–60, 65, 83
    Kit-Kat bar cupcakes, 34–35
    sauces with, 75
    self-frosting cupcakes with, 36–37
    types of, 16
Chocolate and Vanilla Buttercream Frosting,
    59–60
Chocolate Angel Food Cupcakes, 79
Chocolate Cinnamon Frosting, 87
Chocolate Cream Frosting, 53, 65
Chocolate Fudge Frosting, 83, 89
Chocolate Kit Kat Frosting, 35
Chocolate Marshmallow Cupcakes, 54–55

Chocolate Mocha Cupcakes, 122–23
Chocolate Nougat Cake, 80–81
Chocolate Orange Cupcakes, 88–89
Chocolate Spice Cupcakes, 86–87
Citrus Glaze, 127
Cleanup, process of, 29
Coconut
   fillings, 44, 84
   topping, 109–10
Coconut Cream Cheese Filling, 44
Coconut Cream-Filled Chocolate Cupcakes,
   84–85
Coffee cake cupcakes, 105–18
Coloring, food, 24
Cooling cupcakes, 19
Cream (term), 20
Cream cheese
   filling of coconut and, 44
   frosting, 57, 99
Cream-filled cupcakes, 2. *See also* Fillings
Creamy Chocolate Frosting, 43
Creamy Marshmallow Frosting, 55
Crumb Topping, 117
Cupcakes. *See also* Fillings; Frostings;
      Toppings
   baking, with children, 26–29
   baking terms applying to, 20–21
   baking time for, 19
   basic techniques for making, 17–20
   cake recipes adapted for, 2
   children's favorite, 30–60
   chocolate in (*see* Chocolate)
   cooling, 19
   cream-filled, 2
   cupcake liners for baking (*see* Bake
      cups)
   determining doneness of, 12
   dinner party, 61–75
   equipment for baking, 8–12

fat, calories, cholesterol, and sodium in,
   120
freezing, 2, 19–20
frosting and decorating tips, 21–24
fruit in (*see* Fruit)
glazes for, 95, 116, 127
ingredients and chemistry of, 12–17
low-fat, 119–29
nuts in (*see* Nuts)
origin and history of, 4–5
sauce for, 75

Date Nut Cupcakes, 103
Decorating tips, 23–24
Delicious Prune Cupcakes, 113–14
Dinner party cupcakes, 61–75

Easy Carrot Cupcakes, 56–57
Easy Cream Cheese Frosting, 57, 99
Easy Meringue Topping, 101–2
Eggs, 13
   cracked open by children, 28
   separating, 21
Egg whites, 14
Electric mixers, 10–11
Equipment, 8–12
   assembling, 17
Extracts, 15–16

Fanny Merritt Farmer's Boston Cooking-
      School Cook Book, 4
Fats, 14, 120
Fillings. *See also* Frostings; Toppings
   coconut, 84
   coconut cream cheese, 44
   lemon, 100
   peanut-butter, 30
   walnut, 107
Flour, 12–13

Fluted paper baking cups, 4, 9
Fold (term), 20–21
Food colors, 24
Freezing
  cupcakes, 2, 19–20
  frosting, 23
Frostings. *See also* Fillings; Toppings
  basic butter, 85
  buttercream, 81
  butterscotch, 47
  chocolate and vanilla buttercream,
    59–60
  chocolate cinnamon, 87
  chocolate fudge, 83, 89
  chocolate Kit Kat, 35
  chocolate sauce, 75
  colored, 24
  cream cheese, 57, 99
  creamy chocolate, 43
  creamy marshmallow, 55
  for German chocolate cupcakes, 73
  glazes, 95, 116, 127
  maple walnut, 96–97
  meringues, 101–2, 129
  mocha, 123
  orange, 125
  pineapple, 92–93
  rainy day, 41
  root beer float, 49
  self-frosting cupcakes, 36–37
  strawberry cream, 33
  tips on, 21–23
Fruit, 17
  apple nut cupcakes, 111–12
  applesauce cupcakes, 121
  banana nut cupcakes, 98–99
  cherry and chocolate topping, 67
  citrus glaze, 127
  date nut cupcakes, 103

food coloring from, 24
lemon-blueberry cupcakes, 117–18
lemon glaze, 116
lemon lift cupcakes, 126–27
lemon meringue cupcakes, 100–102
orange cupcakes, 44–45, 88–89, 92–93,
  124
orange frosting, 125
orange glaze, 95
pineapple orange cupcakes, 92–93
pineapple topping, 68–69
prune cupcakes, 113–14
strawberry cupcakes, 70–71, 128–29
strawberry frostings, 33, 129

German Chocolate Cupcakes, 72–73
Gingerbread Cupcakes, 63
Glazes
  citrus, 127
  lemon, 116
  orange, 95

Healthy cupcakes, 119–29
Henry's Race Car Cupcakes, 52–53

Ice Cream Cone Cupcakes, 42–43
Ice Cream Sundae Cupcakes, 38–39
Ingredients of cupcakes, 12–17
  blending in sequence, 18
  describing to children, 28
  measuring accurately, 18

Jumbo muffin pans, 8, 9

Kit-Kat Cupcakes, 34–35

Ladles, small, 11, 29
Leavening, 15
Lemon Blueberry Crumb Cupcakes, 117–18

Lemon Filling, 100
Lemon Glaze, 116
Lemon Lifts, 126–27
Lemon Meringue Cupcakes, 100–102
Liners. *See* Bake cups
Liquid measuring cups, 10
Liquids, 13, 28–29
Low-fat cupcakes, 119–29

Magic Self-Frosting Cupcakes, 36–37
Maple Walnut Cupcakes, 96
Maple Walnut Frosting, 96–97
Marble Cupcakes, 64–65
Margarine, 14
Marshmallows, 54–55
Measuring cups, 10
Measuring spoons, 10
Meringues
  easy, 101–2
  strawberry, 129
Mix (term), 21
Mocha Frosting, 123
Motes, Dale, 4
Muffin pans, 8–9
  greasing and flouring, 18
  filling, 19, 23
  positioning, in oven, 19

Nuts, 16–17
  almond and coconut cupcakes, 109–10
  apple nut cupcakes, 111–12
  banana nut cupcakes, 98–99
  date nut cupcakes, 103
  pecan cupcakes, 94–95
  walnut cupcakes, 96–97
  walnut-filled cupcakes, 107–8

Orange cupcakes, 44–45, 88–89, 124–25
Orange Frosting, 125

Orange Glaze, 95
Orange-Glazed Pecan Cupcakes, 94–95
Orange Spice Cupcakes, 124–25
Oven, 11
  positioning muffin pans in, 19
  preheating, 17–18
Oven thermometer, 11, 18

Paper liners. *See* Bake cups
Peanut Butter–filled Chocolate Cupcakes,
  30–31
Pecan cupcakes, 94–95
Perfect Picnic Cupcakes, 44–45
Pineapple Frosting, 92–93
Pineapple Orange Cupcakes, 92–93
Pineapple Topping, 68
Pineapple Upside-Down Cupcakes, 68–69
Pink Princess Cupcakes, 32–33
Poppy Seed Cupcakes, 115–16
Prune cupcakes, 113–14
Pure extracts, 16

Rainy Day Cupcakes, 40–41
Recipes, reviewing, 17
Root Beer Float Cupcakes, 48
Root Beer Float Frosting, 49

Safety concerns, 27
Sauces, bittersweet chocolate, 75. *See also*
  Frostings; Toppings
School Party Cupcakes, 58–60
Separating eggs (term), 21
Shapiro, Jerry, 4
Shortening, 14
Sift (term), 21
Sifter, 10
Sifting flour, 13, 28
Solid measuring cups, 10
Spatulas, 11

Strawberry Cream Frosting, 33
Strawberry Patch Angel Food Cupcakes, 127
Strawberry Patch Meringue, 129
Strawberry Short Cupcakes, 70–71
Sugar, 14–15

Tea Party Miniatures, 50–51
Techniques for baking cupcakes, 17–20
Temperature
   of eggs, 13–14
   of fats, 14
Terminology of baking, 20–21
Texas-style muffin pans, 8, 9
Thermometers, 11
Toppings. *See also* Frostings
   almond-coconut, 109

chocolate and cherry, 67
crumb, 117
ice cream sundae cupcakes, 38–39
meringue, 101–2
pineapple, 68–69
suggestions for, 41
whipped cream, 33

Vanilla extract, 15–16
Vegetable food colors, 24

Walnut-filled Coffee Cupcakes, 107–8
Whip (term), 21
Whipped Cream Topping, 33
Wire racks, 11, 19